KT-226-627

NOTES & QUERIES

compiled by
Brian Whitaker
illustrations by
David Austin

FOURTH ESTATE · *London*

First published in Great Britain by
Fourth Estate Limited
289 Westbourne Grove
London W11 2QA

Copyright © 1990 by Guardian Newspapers Ltd

British Library Cataloguing in Publication Data
Notes and queries
1. Miscellaneous facts
I. Whitaker, Brian II. The Guardian
032.02

ISBN 1-872180-22-1

Typeset in Bodoni by York House Typographic Ltd, Han-
well, London W7
Printed and bound by Clays Ltd, Bungay

NOTES &
QUERIES

PREFACE

IF YOU'RE wondering what this all about, don't scratch your head. Mr Leach of Cambridge will explain why on page 153. Far better to follow Ms Kaye's advice on page 152 and put the kettle on for a cup of tea.

Most of the blame for this infuriating little volume must go to Alan Rusbridger, Features Editor of *The Guardian*. It was his idea to start a weekly column in the newspaper which would answer – or at least try to answer – those niggling questions that are difficult to look up in conventional reference books: a sort of cross between the Brains Trust and Trivial Pursuit. Since *The Guardian* has well over a million regular readers – many of them highly educated – he reasoned that someone among them would be able to provide an answer to virtually any question that other readers dared to ask.

And so it proved. The letters poured in and sometimes, only an hour or two after Notes & Queries had reached the breakfast tables, our fax machine was beeping with readers' answers.

One thing we quickly learned is that *Guardian* readers relish a good argument. Ask a simple question like why water is wet and someone will swear that it isn't wet anyway. Ask why dusters are yellow and psychologists will battle with historians over conflicting theories.

If there's a moral to all this, it's probably that the more sure you are about the answer, the more likely you are to be wrong.

By the way, is the kettle boiling yet? Just be thankful that you're not reading this on Mount Everest. Up there, according to Mr Johnstone of London SE24, boiling water is too cold to make a decent brew.

Brian Whitaker

QUESTION: Who said 'Give me 26 soldiers of lead and I will conquer the world'?

☐ THE actual statement, if history and allegory are correct, was 'Give me 24 soldiers of lead...' It is a reference to the type alphabet of printers before the adoption of U and J, and is claimed to have been said by Johann Gutenberg, who is generally credited with inventing printing from moveable type.

However, because of ligatures and similar printers' characters, and especially because this is all supposed to have taken place in Strasbourg and/or Mainz between 1430 and 1450, it is likely he was setting out to have an army of far more than 26.
David Parkes-Bristow, Harrow, Middx.

QUESTION: Who was Fred Fanackerpan?

☐ HE was the subject of a Gracie Fields song: the unfortunate, gauche young man summoned by Gracie to the ordeal of meeting the family for high tea on Sunday... 'There were aunties and uncles and loads of strawberry jam, All waiting to welcome Fred Fanackerpan.' Needless to say, the last line is... 'And that was the last we saw of Fred Fanackerpan'.
R. E. Mack, E. Finchley, London N2.

☐ THE song featuring this gentleman was certainly sung by Gracie Fields but Fred was not her boyfriend. She states quite definitely at the start: 'There's been a bit of bother with our sister Mary Ann'. This, of course, rhymes with Fanackerpan.

I feel the said Fred may have been a figure of fun in Lancashire a long time before Gracie's song but it was certainly this song which gave the man greater currency.
Terry Mullins, London N7.

QUESTION: What is the name of the neck-flap at the back of the traditional Foreign Legionnaire's cap?

☐ IT IS a havelock (after Sir H. Havelock, general in India, 1795-1857).
Kenneth Simpson, Ashton-under-Lyne, Lancs.

QUESTION: The aerial shot of London used in the introduction to 'EastEnders' – what camera lens was used and from what altitude was it taken?

☐ IT WAS prepared from about 1,000 aerial photographs. The photographs were taken during the summer of 1981 from a height of 2,500 feet using a specialised aerial

survey camera. The camera, which was made in Switzerland, is called a Wild RC8 and weighs approximately 600lb. The camera lens focal length is 6in and the lens alone weighs 75lb. The aerial photography was obtained from a De Havilland DH104 Dove aircraft. The BBC bought a set of photographs from Aerofilms Ltd in 1984 and montaged them together to make the one image used for 'EastEnders'.
R. C. A. Cox, BSc ARICS, Managing Director, Hunting Aerofilms, Boreham Wood, Herts.

QUESTION: Why are car tax discs round?

☐ THEY were made round to be waterproof in the days when they were fixed outside cars (and are still fixed on motorbikes). Before plastic was invented the only logical solution was a circular holder over which a circular glass cover in a metal frame could be screwed into a waterproof seal.
W. W. Bloomfield, Frimley, Camberley, Surrey.

☐ I THINK the answer can be found in Collins' *Concise English Dictionary*, page 215: 'Disc. Any flat, circular thing.'
L. Williamson, Islington, London N7.

QUESTION: What is the name of the slender-necked, bulbous-bottomed flasks filled with coloured liquid in chemists' shop windows?

☐ IN English the name is 'carboy' – which comes from the Persian *quarrabe*. Such *quarrabes* can still be seen in all the bazaars in Iran where herbal distillates are stored. There the bottles, usually green in colour, are covered in basket-work to protect them, rather like a chianti bottle.
(Mrs) P. Salmanpour, Arnside, via Carnforth, Lancs.

QUESTION: What is the title of a novel about an elderly woman determined to reach a blue lake in the Himalayas? She achieved this journey by pony with one Indian servant.

☐ THE story may well be *Ahmed and the Old Lady* by Jon Godden. It was published in New York in 1976 by Alfred A. Knopf.
(Mrs) J. W. Buckley, Banbury, Oxon.

QUESTION: What is the origin of the phrase 'Happy as a sandboy'?

☐ A THIN layer of dry sand was spread each day on the floors of inns, taverns, ale houses, etc, centuries ago to absorb the filth brought in on the footwear of the patrons. This sand carpet was spread by 'sand boys' and was swept up early the following morning before re-sanding. This fouled sand was then taken outside for riddling to separate out anything dropped by the previous day's patrons. You can imagine how delighted the sand boys would be to find the odd golden guinea and anything else of value from the sweepings. Hence the expression.
D. M. Burton, Grimsby, S. Humberside.

☐ IN THE 1840s sand boys could buy two-and-a-half tons of sand for 3s 6d and sell that quantity to all the different establishments and make between £6 and £7 per morning. When sawdust replaced sand in public houses the boys were less than happy.
A. J. Armstrong, Bexhill-on-Sea, E. Sussex.

QUESTION: At the beginning of Luc Besson's film, *Subway*, Christopher Lambert tries various cassettes in his car. What is the music he eventually chooses?

I've seen the film three times and I'm sure it's been changed.

☐ THE music is by the German group, Propaganda. The track is called 'The Murder of Love' and comes from the album, *A Secret Wish*, released by ZTT in 1985. The album is quite wonderful but the group never got the recognition they deserved; although they had a couple of minor hits, the whole ZTT operation at that time was geared more to Frankie Goes to Hollywood. Indeed, this eventually led to the group's demise. Claudia Brücken, the group's singer, went on to form half of ACT, themselves a pale shadow of Propaganda. I wonder whatever happened to Propaganda's other members.
Chris Bailey, Brighton, E. Sussex.

☐ APPARENTLY the original release of the film used a piece called 'Speedway' for the entire chase sequence. This can be found on the soundtrack album, scored by Eric Seera. Later releases (including video) featured music by the German group, Propaganda.
Owen Dixon, Letchworth, Herts.

QUESTION: How do you stop a neighbour's cat scratching up your garden?

☐ CONCRETE one or the other.
A. J. Rimmer, Lytham St Annes.

☐ GET a cat of your own: your cat will keep your neighbour's cat away and will do most his or her own scratching.
Rennie Bere, Bude.

☐ TRY placing discarded light bulbs among the bushes and plants.
M. Thompstone, Bury.

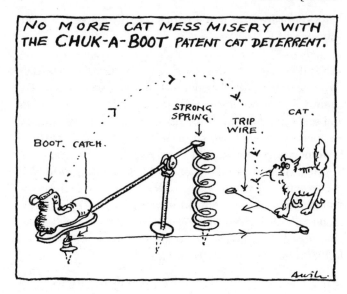

NO MORE CAT MESS MISERY WITH THE CHUK-A-BOOT PATENT CAT DETERRENT.

☐ (a) TRY 'No Mess' made by Vetbed, of Garforth, Leeds. (b) Get a water pistol.
John Douch, MRCVS, Dover.

☐ I AM trying short pieces of holly in the ground.
L. C. Dutton, Rickmansworth.

QUESTION: Can anyone identify the lines: 'Gold begets in Brethrens Hate/Gold in Families Debate;/ Gold does Friendship separate/Gold does Civil Wars create'?

☐ IT WAS written by Abraham Cowley (1618-67).
R. Davies, Tarporley.

QUESTION: Why are the largest insects only a few inches long? Is there any reason why they should not evolve into creatures the size of elephants?

☐ INSECTS are one of several classes of animals belonging to the major group, the Arthropoda (the jointed legged ones). All of these animals have an external jointed skeletal skin which is rather like a hard armour. In order to increase in size, arthropods must periodically shed their skin, a process which renders them vulnerable until the new stretched skin can harden to function again as a skeletal support.

Some arthropods are able to survive many such growth spurts because they live in water which supports the floppy vulnerable stage. But insects which live in air would risk desiccation and collapse under these circumstances. For this reason, most accomplish their growth during a special larval stage and are severely limited in growth once they are adult.

Insects do not have conventional lungs but breathe instead with a system of microscopic pores through which gases diffuse in and out of their bodies. This system would be hopelessly inefficient with much larger body sizes. The reason is because of relative rates at which surface area and volume increase. Consider a one-inch cube which has a surface area of six square inches and a ratio of 6:1. Double the size to a two-inch cube (eight cubic inches) which has a surface area of 24 square inches and a ratio of only 3:1. It becomes clear that the body volume of the animal would be increasing at a rate too fast for the maintenance of an efficient surface-related respiratory mechanism.

This same principle would cause 'design problems' in connection with other aspects of their life processes. Mouth parts of insects are 'designed' specifically according to feeding habit. Enlarging these parts would render them unsuitable for the insect's diet, while keeping them at constant size would prevent the larger animal from acquiring sufficient food. Consider the amount of sap an elephant-sized aphid would need to take through its 'hypodermic' mouth nozzle! To grow a mouth tube with a bigger bore would render it quite unsuited for precision plant puncturing, not to mention the effect on the plant on which the aphid depends.

It is difficult to imagine how some insects could fit a substantially greater growth phase into their lifespan. A butterfly, for example, forms its wings in a once-and-for-all process at the end of metamorphosis. There is no mechanism by which it could grow further, so a larger version would require an already elephant-sized caterpillar which would collapse under its own weight. Some moths are simply a non-feeding, egg-laying stage in the life-cycle of the organism. Their 'purpose' in life is simply to reproduce and ensure the continuity of the species. Apart from the fact that there is no feeding mechanism to provide the necessary energy for growth, there would be no evolutionary advantage since the animal dies after fulfilling its brief reproductive function.

There are more problems. There is a finite limit to the size of any structure constructed out of a given material. This can be illustrated very easily with aluminium kitchen foil. It is easy to construct quite rigid small-scale objects with folded foil but when, with increase in size, the total weight of the structure is too great for the strength of the foil, it will collapse unless a thicker gauge of foil is substituted. Translated into insect terms, a stage would be reached when (say) legs would need to be so thickly built that they would become a clumsy hindrance. *John W. Stanley, Keele University.*

☐ I THINK John Stanley has tended to sell Mother Nature a bit short. Certainly, elephant-sized insects are out, but evolution might well have produced a viable lobster-style land insect, 30 inches long, with a type of air-lung (scorpions have pulmonary sacs with "lung-books"), and feeding lobster-wise by tearing up flesh with its claws and stuffing it into its mouth (might have made a jolly good watchdog?).

Of other insects, way back, there used to be dragon-flies big enough to give a modern kestrel a fright, and arthropoda in the sea (although probably not much good on land) included six-foot-long eurypterids such as Pterygotus anglicus.

Surely, a major reason for today's insects being small is that their size suits the remaining environmental niches now available for such versatile creatures.

L. Clarke, Uxbridge, Middx.

☐ MUCH of John Stanley's exposition is incorrect. Insects lose little water when they moult and (by his own dimensional argument) it is the smallest which are then most at risk through desiccation. Respiration is not limiting. Many insects inspire and expire not unlike ourselves, while some can pump air in at the front and out at the rear end, which is even more efficient. Insect flight muscle respires at a higher rate than any other known tissue.

It is ridiculous to select a particular insect like an aphid or butterfly and say that at elephant size it could not get enough sap or fly. One would not get a viable mouse, if one simply blew it up thirty fold. A beetle's mouth parts are far more efficient than those, for example, of a tortoise, while a bug a few feet long which injects enzymes into its prey and then sucks up the soup could be a formidable predator, protected by far better armour than any present-day carnivore.

On a strength for weight basis, insect wing material is better than that of a bird, and on simple engineering principles, a tube, which is the basis of the insect skeleton, is a more efficient structural member than a solid rod like a bone: it would be better than an elephant's leg at elephant size. And since the insect absorbs most of its skin-skeleton before moulting and re-uses it towards the next one, it is also a very economical system.

By brain transplants, we have successfully made immature insects grow to abnormally large size, including examples of those many insects in which the wings grow appreciably during the larval stage; true if one makes a winged adult grow and moult by such techniques its wings get in a frightful mess, but wingless adults like stick insects naturally go on growing as adults, and the termite queen grows to an emormous size while adult.

The only physical reason we can suggest why the terrestrial insect may be limited in size is that when it moults, it must go through a brief stage when it inflates its gut with air to expand the new skeleton before making it rigid. Could it produce sufficient internal pressure to do so if it were very large? If it immersed itself in water at this stage there would be no problem: crabs and lobsters manage this very well by swallowing water. There are of course a multitude of biological reasons why today's insects are not bigger, the most obvious of which is that they are doing very nicely at their present sizes and there's nothing to be gained by being bigger. But when they inherit the earth, as they undoubtedly will, I for one would not put it beyond them to produce some monsters.
(Sir) James Beament FRS, Queens' College, Cambridge.

□ I WAS taught that the limiting factor for insect growth was respiratory, but I would not contradict Sir James Beament unless his own argument was flawed.

He suggests that the moulting insect inflates its gut with air to stretch the new exoskeleton, thus limiting the insect's size because the larger the gut, the more effort is required to inflate it. This is not so, as any anaesthetist will tell you.

The pressure within an inflated elastic container is related *directly* to the tension in the wall of the container and *inversely* to the radius. This is Laplace's Law and is familiar to anaesthetists because it is important to respiratory physiology. The obvious result is that as an inflated container grows bigger, the pressure required to inflate it becomes *smaller*, to the limit of the elasticity of the container. Anyone blowing up a balloon experiences this: the extreme effort to start, followed by an easy inflation. The balloon becomes more difficult to inflate beyond a certain point, but only because it has reached the limit of its elasticity.

Other phyla have evolved creatures of all sizes at some time in history, but not insects. Sir James's gut-inflating insects would have it easier as they grew bigger, assuming that their gut grew with them, so there must be some other factor which prevents them growing.

John R. Davies, FFARCS (Consultant Anaesthetist), Lancaster.

□ JOHN Davies is of course correct that the pressure drops as you inflate a balloon, and likewise inside an insect each time it blows itself up when it moults. The factor Mr Davies has overlooked is that an insect moults many times and the walls of its 'balloon', i.e. its external skeleton, must be thicker every time. Indeed, suppose by moulting a few times it doubles in length, it becomes eight times heavier; its skeleton must then be about four times as thick to support this weight after it has inflated itself. So the pressure needed to start inflating the skeleton at each moult goes up steeply with size. The same argument defeats the saying: 'If a flea was as big as an elephant it could jump over the Houses of Parliament', because weight increases as the cube of length, whereas muscle force only as the square.

(Sir) James Beament, Queens' College, Cambridge.

QUESTION: Who was Sephestra in Robert Greene's poem, 'Sephestra's Lullaby', in the *Oxford Book of English Verse*?

□ SEPHESTIA (not Sephestra) is a character in Robert Greene's romance, *Menaphon,* published in 1589.

Banished by her father, Damocles, Sephestia lives in disguise with a group of shepherds and adopts the name Samela. In a very convoluted story the beautiful Samela is courted in turn by the shepherd Menaphon, her father Damocles, her husband Melicertus – whom she believed had been lost in a shipwreck – and even her son, Pleusidippus, who had been captured by pirates in his infancy.
David Young, Bingham, Nottingham.

QUESTION: If sugar is bad for you, how come hummingbirds can eat nothing else?

☐ SUGAR is also bad for hummingbirds. Have you ever seen one with a full set of teeth?
B. White, Preston, Lancs.

QUESTION: How large is the Jewish population in the USSR?

☐ THE *Encyclopaedia Britannica* 1989 Yearbook says 1.1 per cent of the Soviet population are of Jewish religious affiliation. In 1988 the USSR's total population was 285,796,000 – which gives 3,143,756.
Arthur Clifford, Southall, Middx.

QUESTION: Could somebody please confirm that (a) when Bill and Ben went through the hole at the back of the chicken shed a little man was sometimes seen in the wood and (b) a shy white squirrel appeared occasionally?

☐ THE little man was known as Dan, Dan, the Potato Man, as he was made out of potatoes joined together. He was fond of singing a potato-man song and doing a little

dance while Bill and Ben clapped behind him. The white squirrel was seen very rarely, and would sit in a black umbrella.
Kath Brown, Grays, Essex.

□ MY grandpa bought me a video of Bill and Ben, and the white squirrel appears in a story about some musical vegetables. The squirrel only eats beans.
Hannah Boulton (aged 2½) per grandpa, Macclesfield, Cheshire.

QUESTION: Can anyone give a clue as to the situation which gave rise to the signal (I believe a naval signal) which was worded approximately thus: 'Render all aid short of actually helping'?

□ I HAVE always assumed that the phrase was originally applied to the assistance provided to us by the Americans before they were themselves attacked at Pearl Harbor.
Pat Paget, Manchester 20.

QUESTION: Can anybody identify the cat-hating old man in fiction who used to go around saying: 'There are no cats in the Bible'?

□ THE old man is Andrew Vessons, and he occurs in Mary Webb's *Gone to Earth*, published by Cape in 1917: 'Sitting at the supper ...' said Hazel ... 'and the old servant hopping to and agen like thrussels after worms.' 'Thrussel yourself!' muttered Andrew ... He retired again, remarking to the cat in a sour lugubrious voice, as he always did when ruffled, 'There's no cats i' the Bible' (Chapter 5).

Incidentally, Vessons is nowhere stated to hate cats; he is just a curmudgeonly old bachelor.
Judith Dutton, Ellesmere Port, South Wirral.

QUESTION: On a school trip to the Festival of Britain in 1951 I played the game Nim against an early computer. Although I have asked at the Science Museum, I have never been able to find which computer it was.

☐ IT WAS the Ferranti Nimrod computer, which was certainly at one time in the Science Museum, where I saw it and bought the booklet (priced at one shilling and sixpence) which Ferranti produced to go with it. Its main store – what would now be called its RAM – was used only for the data involved in playing Nim, and had a total capacity of five 3-bit words (values from 0 to 7) and eight 2-bit words (values from 0 to 3). It was quite a large affair – 12ft x 5ft x 9ft, using about 350 valves.

An unusual feature was that numbers in binary form were not represented dynamically, as was then the rule, by trains of binary pulses in continuous motion, but statically as two-level voltages – as is now universally the case.

It is now largely forgotten what pioneers Ferranti were in those days; nearly all their machines – Pegasus, Mercury and finally Atlas in particular – were all far ahead of their time.
Benedict Nixon, Muswell Hill, London N10.

☐ IT WAS not really a computer at all; this device could do nothing but play Nim. It consisted of a number of relays mounted on perspex panels, so that they could be clearly seen operating. From three rows of coloured lights (containing six, five and three respectively) a maximum of three were extinguished from any one row by the machine and a visitor in turn; the aim being to try to avoid removing the last one.

The machine always won against an opponent who elected to make the first move. To beat it, one needed to know the winning strategy and allow the machine to

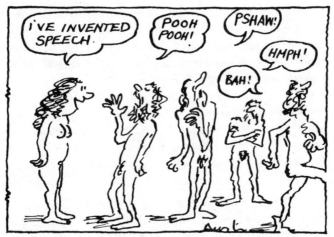

start. I was 16 in 1951 and spent long hours trying (in vain) to win.
Len Johnson, W. Malvern, Worcs.

QUESTION: **It is generally accepted that human speech progressed from inarticulate sounds via onomatopoeic sounds to coherent speech. How is it that the presumed simple language developed into strictly formalised languages like Classical Greek and Latin when the general tendency since then has been towards a breakdown of formality? This is particularly obvious in English.**

☐ THE onomatopoeic or 'bow-wow' theory of how speech developed is no longer accepted. It is most probable that humans first had a system of communication by gestures (similar to that of present-day chimpanzees), and that speech began as a back-up to this gesture system. All this probably took place between 50,000 BC and 30,000 BC; the oldest recorded languages (5,000 to 6,000 years ago) were no less complex than those of the present day.

The difference between Latin and English, say, is not
in complexity but in type of grammatical system. Grammar shows the relationship between the items in a sentence; Latin, like Russian and Old English, encoded this
information in suffixes (the -ae in feminae meant 'feminine' and 'of'), whereas English, like Chinese, prefers to
use individual particles ('of the woman') coupled with
strict word-order (contrast 'Dog bites man' and 'Man
bites dog'!) to show the same information.

*Francis R. Jones, The Language Centre, University of
Exeter.*

☐ FRANCIS Jones somewhat oversimplifies the 'origin of
language' question. The theory that it arose as an ampli-
fication of gestural language is itself a minority position
now, notwithstanding the eminence of its main advocate
(Gordon W. Hewes). As far as I can see there is total
disarray on the question regarding timing (early, i.e. pre-
1 million years; late – c. 50,000 years and very late – c.
15,000 years), source (vocal vs gestural) and primary
function (social/emotional vs intellectual/problem-
solving).

Also, of course, it is far from clear what level of
complexity is to count as equivalent to modern human
language. This argument will, as they say, run and run ...
Anyone seriously wishing to get embroiled in the debate
might be interested in contacting the Language Origins
Society, c/o Prof Jan Wind, Dept of Human Genetics,
Free University, POB7161, 1007 MC Amsterdam.

*Graham Richards, Senior Lecturer, Dept. of Psychology,
Polytechnic of East London.*

☐ CASE endings are only one of the ways in which
languages can express such notions as possession, location or subject versus object. Other alternatives include
the use of fixed word-order patterns or independent
words such as prepositions and adverbs. A particular
language can use more than one of these resources simul-

taneously. It's true that Latin makes more use of endings than English and than its direct descendants such as French, Spanish or Italian. On the other hand, these modern languages make more use of prepositions and fixed word-order patterns than Latin.

Over time, word endings can get worn away by sound change. However, this doesn't mean that all language change involves an inexorable march away from case ending patterns. Endings themselves typically develop historically from independent words such as adverbs which, through time, become directly incorporated in the words they originally stood next to.

These changes tend to happen cyclically over a long period. For example, we can sometimes reconstruct a series of developments in which an adverb becomes attached to a neighbouring word and is then eroded away; at the same time its function is taken over by some alternative resource, such as a particular word-order pattern or some other word.

John Harris, Department of Phonetics and Linguistics, University College, London.

QUESTION: Does anyone have evidence suggesting that sheep tend to give birth when the tide is high in coastal regions?

☐ ACCORDING to folklore, births occur when the tide comes in, and deaths when the tide goes out. When I was a junior doctor in a busy maternity department in a coastal town I tested this belief. I sought out the times of all births in a two-month period and checked them against tide tables. Any births that were induced, as well as those delivered by Caesarian section, were discarded. The results did not support folk belief. Fifty per cent were born when the tide was coming in, and 50 per cent when the tide was going out. There seemed no difference in the

mortality of the two groups. I doubt if sheep differ from humans in respect of birth rhythms.
Margaret Millard, MD, Painswick, Glos.

☐ AN obstetrician in London has, within the last two or three years, published a paper on the relationship between high tide and human deliveries. The paper, published in the *British Medical Journal*, was inconclusive in its findings.
(Dr) Peter Glanvill, Chard, Somerset.

☐ THE goatkeeper's bible, *Goat Husbandry*, by David Makenzie, says: 'Like sheep, goats seem able to postpone or accelerate the birth of their kids to take advantage of good weather; older goats use their discretion in the matter more notably than first kidders.

   'The first good kidding day which comes within the fortnight in which the kids are due is the normal choice of an experienced mother. A good kidding day is a mild and humid one with a minimum of wind; lambs and kids are best born in a Scotch mist, where loss of heat by evaporation of the natal slime is at a minimum.' So the goat and the sheep it seems, are rather superior to humans in this respect.
Stephen Abrahall, Shepton Mallet, Somerset.

QUESTION: My friends are always asking why I am nicknamed 'Nobby' Clarke. Can anyone help?

☐ THE explanation offered by my father (born 1881) was that in his youth clerks habitually wore top hats to work. Working folk rated them as 'nobs' – implying a blend of irony and scoffing, since real 'nobs' (i.e. upper class men) did not work in such a humble capacity. Soon everyone with this surname came to be nicknamed 'Nobby'.
A. Whigham Price, Durham.

☐ IN pre-war days, British troops stationed in India learned a few words of Urdu, such as *dhobi* (laundry); *chota* (small); *burra* (large); *pawni* (water). The Urdu for clerk (office variety) is *nobbi*, hence a soldier named 'Clarke' was nicknamed Nobby. Similarly a soldier whose name was 'Wood' would be called 'lakri' which was/is the Urdu for 'wood'. I can't guarantee the spelling of the Urdu words, having only heard them spoken.
George Richardson, St Austell, Cornwall.

QUESTION: Does anyone remember those devices advertised a few years ago that were supposed to turn old newspapers into burnable briquets? If so, where can I get one?

☐ MY advice is don't make briquets out of old newspapers – I did. I had several buckets of stinking sludge in my cellar. Ladling this horrible grey sludge into the squeezer and applying nine stones of pressure produced sludge all over everything and a wad of **** words fail me. This wad sat on the radiator for two or three weeks before it was dry enough to burn. The horrible smell permeated the house.

The chore of making these wads became an unpleasant bi-weekly necessity – having bought the gadget and saved the newspapers, I was bound to do it. But the real problem turned out to be the unburnability of the briquets. They smouldered in a resentful sour way, sending up dense clouds of acrid smoke, and left a flaky residue. So I repeat: DON'T.
Christine Fremantle, Battersea, London SW11.

☐ IT'S a messy, time-consuming business of doubtful value. Even if you're prepared to wait five years to recover in terms of fuel value the money spent on the briquet-maker, you have to convert at least 200 pages of newsprint every day of the year. It takes about 150 hours to do it.

The briquets don't pack tightly, and they're at different stages of drying in separate piles, and drying can take a long time. They must be under cover, so be prepared to move your car out of the garage permanently. I know, I tried it.

Far better to send the money straight to Friends of the Earth, give the newspapers to the local church for recycling and give 150 hours per year of your time to an environmentally acceptable cause.
Alan Mackley, Halesworth, Suffolk.

QUESTION: I wish to trace a short story, American I think, which starts: 'Mr — lifted the lid of the dustbin and looked out.'

☐ IT WAS the winner in a 'first sentence' competition in, I think, *Argosy* magazine about 1958. The runner-up was: 'What are you doing in my bath playing with the rubber duck?' she screamed. 'I'm from the ministry,' he said.
Rab Mooney, Ealing, London W5.

☐ IN, I think, the 1930s, a Mr L. Du Gard Peach — possibly a teacher of English — wrote a book on the art of short story writing, in which he gave the quotation as an example of a very telling and arresting opening sentence. I don't remember whether he was quoting from an existing short story or whether he had made the sentence up himself. I have searched through all the *Who's Who*s relevant to the 1930s onwards but can't find a single entry for Mr Du Gard Peach but he was quite a well-known writer about that time.
Miss D. M. Ridehalgh, Blackpool, Lancs.

QUESTION: What is the meaning of the word 'Moby' in Moby Dick?

☐ MELVILLE based his fictional Moby Dick on a real whale popularly called Mocha Dick which terrorised the whalers of the Pacific in the early nineteenth century. He may well have heard of this white monster while working as a harpooner on the whaler *Acushnet*. It seems likely that he did read Joseph Reynold's article, 'Mocha Dick, or the White Whale of the Pacific' in the *Knickerbocker Magazine* of May 1839. The Mocha in Mocha Dick derived from the island of Mocha off the Chilean coast where he had been encountered in 1810.

Why Melville changed the whale's name to Moby has never been satisfactorily explained. There seems to be no evidence of this name before his book. One theory suggests that Melville's tendency to use Biblical names (Ahab, Ishmael, etc) may mean that Moby derives from Moab, son of Lot by his elder daughter (Genesis xix, 37).
D. Young, Nottingham.

☐ IN 1846, four years before the publication of his masterpiece, Melville met up with Richard Tobias Green, with whom he had sailed the South Seas in the early 1840s. Dick Toby: Toby Dick? It is not inconceivable that 'Moby' was derived from a combination of Mocha and Toby.
Michael Pearce, Edinburgh.

QUESTION: Why is the delicious homity – or hommity – pie so called?

☐ COULD it be hominy? – maize, hulled or hulled and crushed with water, a kind of corn porridge (American Indian origin).
M. J. Buniak, London E11.

QUESTION: Why is New York known as the Big Apple?

☐ THE Big Apple was a bar on 42nd Street in New York which was much used by jazz musicians in the Twenties. When musicians bumped into each other while touring in the States they would always arrange to meet up again in the Big Apple, and in time this became synonymous with New York City.
Sharon Simpson, London W14.

☐ THE city of New York for many years has had a large Spanish-speaking population. It is said that one member of this population saw the city (Manhattan in particular) as one large city block – 'una manzana grande'. In Spanish manzana also means 'apple'.
Rick Holland, Cheadle Hulme, Cheshire.

☐ THE explanation that I once heard is that in the 1920s and 1930s jazz musicians in America referred to engagements in large towns and cites as 'a bite of the apple'. The largest city and most prestigious venue was New York – hence the Big Apple.
Arthur Hasler, London N22.

☐ TO THE early Protestant settlers in rural America, urban New York, with its confidence men and painted ladies, was seen as a den of sin and temptation which threatened their new Garden of Eden. Hence 'The Big Apple'.
Simon Bendle, Upminster, Essex.

☐ THE Big Apple was one of the many dances which proliferated during the 1920s and 1930s. It first appeared in New York about 1935.
Munroe Hall, Bury, Lancs.

☐ AS A born and bred New Yorker, I never heard New

York city referred to as the Big Apple before the mid-Seventies. At that time, New York City was bankrupt. Businesses were moving out and tourism was plummeting. It was in the course of the expensive publicity campaign designed to improve the city's image that the phrase first came into common use. Why the 'Big Apple'? Well, New York (the state) was at the time the country's biggest producer of the fruit. Patrons of supermarkets all over America were familiar with 'New York Apples'. Thus the slogan 'New York City – the Big Apple' was developed to sell the city to middle America. New Yorkers, of course, never use the phrase.

Maureen Basedow, W. Germany.

QUESTION: Do ants sleep?

☐ YES, they do – but not in the sense we understand sleep. Research conducted by James and Cottell into sleep patterns of insects (1983) showed that ants have a cyclical pattern of resting periods which each nest as a group observes, lasting around eight minutes in any 12-hour period. Although this means two such rest periods in any 24-hour period, only one of the rest periods bears any resemblance to what we would call sleep. Mandible and antennae activity is at a much lower level (usually up to 65 per cent lower) than during the other rest period in one 24-hour period, indicating a much deeper 'resting' phase.

Basing and McCluskey in 1986 used brain activity recorders on black, red, and soldier ants to determine whether the deeper resting period constituted actual 'sleep'. A steep decline in brain wave fluctuations supported the 'sleep' hypothesis in black and red ants, but surprisingly showed a higher level of brain activity in soldier ants in a deep resting phase.

Kathleen Thorpe, London SW11.

QUESTION: What is the significance of the bees upon the breasts of the female figures on the lower part of the four columns supporting the canopy over the dais on which the Pope sits to receive public audience in St Peter's Church in the Vatican?

☐ THE BEES are the heraldic symbol of the Barberini family to which Pope Urban VIII belonged. He both commissioned and consecrated the great altar canopy or baldacchino of St Peter's. The story goes that the Pope commissioned the baldacchino as a thank-offering for the safe survival of a favourite niece who nearly died in childbirth. This explains the large-bellied appearance of the woman and the distress on her face which increases from column to column until the last, which depicts instead the smiling face of her baby.

The bees thus represent a spot of self-glory for the papal uncle while preserving the modesty of his niece.
Father Robert Davies, Frimley, Surrey.

☐ IT IS said that Bernini, in carving them, was making a comment on the Pope's love life. The shields are shaped to look like the belly of a woman, and the faces depict pleasure, then ecstasy and finally relaxation.
Geoffrey Denton, Chester-le-Street, Co Durham.

QUESTION: I am being driven nuts by a snatch of piano music from Hitchcock's film, *Rope*. I suspect it might be Debussy or Satie. It is played two or three times by one of the murderers in the film.

☐ THE music was by Leo F. Forbstein, based on the theme Perpetual Movement No 1 by Francis Poulenc.
Barry Avery, Kingston, Surrey.

☐ IT IS the first (*Assez modéré*) of Poulenc's 3 *Mouvements Perpetuels*. Hitchcock's choice was apt and

*Bernini's bees: coded comment on a pope's
love life?*

witty, not least in its reference to the constant movement
of the camera – as well as the set and props – required by
his experiment with the 10-minute take.
V. F. Perkins, Joint School of Film and Literature, University of Warwick.

QUESTION: Information wanted on the two songs, 'Lord of the Dance' and 'The Holly and the Ivy', please. When were they written, who wrote them and are either of them based on traditional folk songs or melodies?

☐ 'LORD of the Dance' is a modern song, written in 1963 by Sydney Carter. The tune is a traditional melody, an old Shaker tune called 'Gift To The Simple' which he arranged and adapted. The theme of the words is an ancient one, expressing a similar concept to that of the medieval carol, 'Tomorrow Shall Be My Dancing Day'.

'The Holly and the Ivy' is an English traditional carol. Both words and music of the version which is generally sung were collected from Chipping Campden in Gloucestershire by Cecil Sharp. The holly and ivy are part of the ancient symbolism for male and female, the 'merry organ' is referred to by Chaucer in the 'Nonnes Preestes Tale' and was a portative organ. There are folk singers of today who still use more modern versions, pumped by laborious feet.

Ali Rowe, Carillyon Folk Duo, Evesham, Worcs.

☐ ACCORDING to the *Oxford Book of Carols* the words and tune of 'The Holly and the Ivy' were first taken down and published by Cecil Sharp, early this century, in *English Folk Carols* (Novello). His sources were Mrs Clayton from Chipping Campden and Mrs Wyatt from East Harptree, although the subject-matter must originate from pre-Christian times.

Bill Thomas, Whitefield, Manchester.

☐ 'LORD of the Dance' is a Christianised version of a pagan song. In pagan traditions the horned god (Pan/ Herne the Hunter) is the lord of the spiral dance of Life, Death and Rebirth presided over by the goddess (Diana/ Cerndwen/Brigantia).

E. Bennett, Reading, Berks.

QUESTION: Are the vapours one smells on British Rail 125 trains when they brake as harmless as British Rail tells us?

☐ BR 125 vapours come from the brake blocks (who on earth would put an air intake for the ventilation system near the braking system?) and almost certainly contain cancer-causing benzopyrenes and asbestos.
A. J. P. Dalton, Kentish Town, London.

☐ WHILE undoubtedly unpleasant, the smells are not thought to be harmful. When the disc brakes are applied they generate temperatures in the range of 300°C to 500°C and, as the binding agent which makes the train stop is rubber based, a smell is thereby caused. However, when the brakes are applied, a flap should cover the air-conditioning intake, but if this does not work the smell will persist.
Brian Perren, Potters Bar, Herts.

☐ YOUR correspondent raises the hoary chestnut of high speed train brakes. I can assure him and your other readers that the air conditioning intakes are closed during braking, so the majority of any smell that enters carriages comes through open windows at the ends of the vehicles or through the connections between the coaches. As to the fumes emitted when the brakes are applied, we have satisfied both ourselves and the Health and Safety Executive that they constitute no hazard to the health of our customers or anyone else.
(Dr) M. J. Andrews, Director, Occupational Health and Safety, British Railways Board, London NW1.

☐ OK, we agree that the design of the ventilation system was incompetent. But are the fumes harmful or are they not? They don't smell like rubber to me.
Sam Harrison, Oxford.

QUESTION: Which Roman numerals for 1990 are correct ... MXM, MCMXC, MDCCCCXC or MCMLXXXX or some permutation?

☐ BECAUSE of the way Roman numerals are built up, there is no set way of representing a certain number. As a 'rule of thumb', you shouldn't use more than three of the same together. For example XXX is fine to represent 30, but XXXX is not used for 40 (XL would be better here). This is because of the 'ten before' system in Roman numerals. By putting a lower value numeral before a higher value numeral, we are effectively saying 'this many before'. For example IX means one before ten, which is 9. So, in this case MCMLXXXX wouldn't be used. Also, MDCCCCXC wouldn't be used. In fact this hasn't been used since the 1800s. This, of course, leaves MXM and MCMXC. It doesn't really matter which one you choose, but 'ten before a thousand' isn't usually used. So, I would use MCMXC. But this is only my opinion!
Dean Garraghty, Doncaster.

☐ ROBY'S *Latin Grammar for Schools*, Chapter X, is probably as good a guide as any to classical (Augustan) usage, and he gives some forms like IIC for 98 which are entirely out of use now. My judgement of usage over the last century or so is that the 'subtractive' forms like IV should only be used with one symbol preceding another of value not more than ten times as great; and they are then favoured but not essential. This would allow CM for 900 but not XM for 990. So I would use MCMXC for preference, but regard MDCCCCLXXXX as quite acceptable if I wanted to fill up more space (which is why clockmakers prefer IIII to IV in general). MDCCCCXC has some classical basis, as Roby gives only DCCCC and not CM, but MCMLXXXX would be a little eccentric.
George Toulmin, Cheltenham, Glos.

QUESTION: On frosty mornings, the quickest and most efficient method of cleaning ice from car windows is to use a kettle of lukewarm water. Some people tell me I am asking for trouble in the form of cracking glass; others swear by the method. Can modern glass stand this?

☐ YOU won't crack the glass. Over 20 years (and at least 20 cars) we have applied hot (though not actually boiling) water round all the glass, often two kettlefuls for a large car and thick frost. Two generous applications all round helps warm up the glass and prevents immediate re-icing. Thaw the wipers too. We were sceptical at first, but the method reached us via an ex-Land Rover/Patent Agent, and he knew what he was talking about.
Pauline Holdsworth, Rugby.

QUESTION: When did the distillation of spirits begin? The technology required is reasonably advanced but not, I would have thought, beyond the reach of some of the ancient civilisations. Yet, all the references in the surviving literature appear to be to wine and beer.

☐ THE process may date back to early Alexandrian times (1st century AD). Arab chemists greatly improved the still and used it for large-scale distillation of perfume. The first preparation of strong spirits of wine was made in twelfth-century Europe probably at Salerno medical school, accidentally, in the course of some medical preparation.

The great demand for spirits came with the Black Death in the fourteenth century, hence the name 'aqua vitae'. In the sixteenth century, distillers around Cognac discovered that a second distillation, with ageing in wood, smoothed out the harshness of the drink and made it

pleasant as well as stupefying. In Scotland and Ireland, barley liquor was double-distilled to 'uisge beatha' (Gaelic, later anglicised as 'whisky').
M. J. Hunter, Edinburgh.

QUESTION: What was Bodie's first name in the television series, 'The Professionals'? Did he, in fact, have one?

☐ IN ONE of the books from the series, called *Hunter Hunted,* there is a story centred around a hearing into the death of a suspect while in CI5's custody; the suspected cause of death is a punch delivered by Ray Doyle. Bodie's four Christian names are mentioned – William Philip Andrew Charles ('I was such a regal baby ') in this story, although the general idea in the series was that Bodie would only ever answer when called 'Bodie'.
Paul Gillooly, North Weald, Essex.

QUESTION: Can anyone confirm that when Marco Polo returned to Italy from Japan he brought back a wheat-based noodle called Udon which evolved into what is now known as spaghetti? Also, how did spaghetti get its name?

☐ NO ONE can confirm what Marco Polo brought back from Japan because he never went there. Your reader is confusing China with Japan – as the Japanese warlords did in the 1930s. Marco Polo set out from Venice for Cathay in 1275, a 3,000-mile journey. He returned 20 years later with bags of jewels and spices (worth their weight in gold) and a letter to the Pope that the Kublai Khan had asked him to deliver to his counterpart in the Mysterious West. Marco did not set out without other

provisions, but if they included a bag of Chinese noodles, the bag was probably empty long before his camel had clocked 1,000 miles. At least one document by an Italian friar, pre-dating Marco's return, tells how to prepare lasagna, the flat sheets of dough that had been baked in the sun. It soon became the fast food of the Middle Ages. It could be kept for months and required little fuel to make it edible. It was the grandmother of all pastas. I have seen spaghetti 'evolve into' a mass of soggy noodles by the cook's failure to stir 'the little pieces of string'. Spaghetti comes from the Italian word for string ('spago').
G. Armstrong, Rome.

☐ IN *The Travels* (Penguin edition) Marco Polo discussed the use of cereals in Tartar and Chinese diet and writes of wheat that 'such of it as they harvest they eat only in the form of noodles and other pasty foods'. This, of course, does not prove that Marco Polo brought noodles back with him but a little stretch of the imagination could link the Japanese Soba, or buckwheat noodles, with the first three letters of SPAghetti. More prosaically, Chambers explains the derivation of the word thus: the plural of spaghetto, diminutive of spago, a cord.
David Mackness, Ipswich, Suffolk.

QUESTION: What is the origin of the system of counting that is, as far as I can gather, peculiar to the French? No other language I know counts from sixty through to sixty-nineteen, then on from four-twenties to four-twenties-nineteen.

☐ FRENCH is not the only language which shows remnants of an earlier system of counting in 20s. In Irish, 40 is *da fichit* (2 x 20), 60 is *tri fichit* (3 x 20), and so on. In Danish, 60 is *tre-sind-styve* (3 x 20); 80 is *fir-sind-styve*. Curiously, 50 (*halv-tre-sind-styve*), 70 (*halv-fir-sind-*

styve) and 90 (*halv-fem-sind-styve*) all use half multiples of 20.

The oldest written evidence of a 20 count in Europe is probably the 1050 AD inventory of an English monastery which lists items in both Latin and the vernacular: *V scora scoep* (5 x 20 sheep) *VIII scora oecer* (8 x 20 acres).

Looking at languages with a strong 20 count, such as Basque, suggests that the practice continued from a more ancient language spoken in Europe before the Celtic period and before the spread of the Indo-European family of languages. Why 20? The origin is likely to have been the number of fingers and toes. Evidence of early 20-counts can be found in Central and North America, West Africa and Greenland, as well as Western Europe. However, it is no accident that the majority of counting in the world is in base 10. The 10 digits on our hands are the most accesssible aids for counting. Early Eskimos might have used their toes as well as their fingers. Did they get frost-bite? Or did they carry their 20-count from Asia long before the spread there of the Chinese base 10?
Nigel Langdon, Cameroon.

□ THE system of counting in 20s is also used by the Scots and Manx Gaelic, Welsh, Cornish and Breton. Cornish employs 20s to count up to 200 but the thing being counted remains singular. Thus 179 mice becomes 19 mouse and eight score.
Colin Ellis, Truro, Cornwall.

□ A RESIDUE of the old European preference for counting in 20s is still preserved in the English 20 fluid ounces to the pint, 20 hundredweight to the ton, 20 quires to the ream, and, until recently, 20 shillings to the pound. Twenty is vastly superior to 10 as a base as it has a higher number of denominators. For example, it may be divided into quarters and still produce whole numbers.
H. J. Nicholson, Kettering, Northants.

□ THE French counting system was orginally 'normal', i.e. linguistically logical words for 70, 80 and 90 (*septante, octante, nonante*). The former and latter are still current in Belgium and Switzerland, while the second survives in Swiss French. I suspect they fell out of use in France because they lacked sonority.
Adrian Murphy, London SE16.

QUESTION: Why, precisely, 78, 45, 33 and 16?

□ THE choice of 78 rpm for turntable speeds (or occasionally 80 rpm and other variants, indicated on the label) was an early compromise between a faster speed – of say 100 rpm – which gave superior sound quality (but with a correspondingly shorter playing time) and an equally randomly chosen slower speed of 40 rpm. Early hand-cranked machines were most comfortably operated at a speed of around 80 turns per minute. With the introduction of electrically-powered machines, a motor designed to run at 3,600 revolutions per minute and utilising a 46:1 gear ratio gave a speed of 78.26 – close enough to the old randomly chosen speeds of between 75 and 85 rpm. The choice between 33⅓ and 45 was the result of a battle between rivals RCA and Columbia (CBS) to develop a micro-groove, longer playing record. Unwilling to co-operate, they developed their own separate systems. (Remember cassettes versus cartridges; four quadrophonic sound systems; Betamax versus VHS; Sky versus BSB?) By the mid-Fifties, most major companies were offering both – the 45 for popular repertoire and the 33⅓ for classical music. At half the latter's speed, the 16⅔ was reserved for the spoken world only, and died an early death.
Malcolm Jones, Wimbledon, London SW19.

□ THESE numbers are not multiples of each other.

Therefore their harmonic frequencies do not coincide. Each doubling of frequency halves the amplitude in their electronic waveform so the resonances do not interfere until 16 times 78, for example. By which time the energy levels are so small it hardly matters anyway. Quite useful in things like gramophone records, vehicle body shells, precision oscillators and whatnot.

Lyndon Elias (Eng Tech; AMIElecIE), Didcot, Oxon.

QUESTION: If water is composed of hydrogen and oxygen atoms, why will it not burn?

☐ THE hydrogen and oxygen atoms have already 'burned' to form the chemical compound 'water'. In other words, the atoms are in a state of chemical combination, each water molecule having two hydrogen and one oxygen nuclei in close proximity, surrounded by ten electrons in a stable configuration similar to that of the inert gas, neon. Of these ten electrons, eight are contributed by the oxygen atom, the remaining two coming from the hydrogen atoms to form a complete outer shell of eight electrons, surrounding a complete inner shell of two electrons. To understand why such a system should be highly stable one needs to know something of quantum mechanics, a mathematical theory which is impossible to explain in a few lines.

The results of this theory, however, show that chemical combination tends to occur in such a way that the resulting molecules have electronic structures which approximate to those of the inert gases – helium, neon, argon, krypton, xenon, and so on, as we used to be taught at school. The closer the electron structure of an atom or molecule aproximates to one of these, the more stable it is likely to be – and conversely, atoms or molecules with incomplete outer shells will react with other atoms or

molecules if by doing so the result will be a molecule with an electronic structure closer to that of an inert gas.
H. Pursey, New Malden, Surrey.

□ WATER does not burn because it is not composed of hydrogen and oxygen atoms, but of hydrogen and oxygen ions. By the same token, common salt is benign, and often sprinkled on to boiled eggs, though the elements from which its ions come, sodium (which explodes when dropped into warm water) and chlorine (a greenish-yellow gas used to kill in the First World War) would not be welcome on the breakfast table.
Roger Pearce, Milton Keynes.

QUESTION: Why is sex rampant in the living world? In the species in which it is the norm, what evolutionary advantage does it confer over asexual reproduction – e.g. budding?

□ SEXUAL reproduction probably arose in bacteria some three to four billion years ago to help with repair and deletion of genetic material damaged by the ultraviolet light in an earth as yet unprotected by an ozone layer. Fusions were uneven, one cell squirted its genes into another, and cannibalism was rife. In multicellular forms sexual reproduction appeared perhaps for similar reasons, i.e. to enable the organisms to cope with hostile and changing environments by speeding up genetic variation.

A more recent theory suggests that sex arose to enable the multicellular organism to keep pace with its parasites. These, be they viruses, bacteria, protozoa, etc, have a much shorter reproductive cycle than does the host and so could evolve to overcome the latter's immune system and lead to its extinction – a state of affairs which would benefit neither party. Sexual reproduction speeds up variation in the host's offspring to prevent this from occurring. Co-evolution of host and parasite is a carefully regulated process, and even the terrible epidemics of the past did not wipe out the whole population as the host eventually develops immunity. The virus may go on to develop a new antigenic form and the interaction starts again.

There is increasing evidence that genetic and hormonal interactions in the developing foetus play some part in shaping sexual, cognitive and behavioural patterns in the future adult. Not only can many of the male and female differences in cognition and sexuality be explained by these processes, but aspects of variant sexuality, e.g. homosexuality, have been elucidated. Having individuals with such differences enables a much wider plasticity of thought and behaviour which in evolutionary terms cannot but be beneficial.

(Dr) Raymond Goodman, Hope Hospital, Salford, Manchester.

QUESTION: How and when did the American accent become recognisably American?

☐ THE divergence is due to a series of sound changes which has taken place since English was first established in the New World. Contrary to popular belief, these innovations have mostly affected British pronunciation. One example is the loss of the original R-sound from certain parts of words, as in cart, bird. The spelling reflects the older R-ful pattern which is maintained in what has come to be known as General American English. Another British innovation is the back or 'broad' pronunciation of the A-sound in words such as bath and dance. Most varieties of American English retain an older front sound.

In making these comparisons, it's as well to remember that both British and American accents are quite heterogeneous. For example, although R-dropping is now normal in standard British usage, Scottish and some regional English dialects share with General American the retention of the original R-sound. Conversely, some regional American varieties are R-less.

Virtually all of the recent changes in standard British pronunciation have been adopted from south-eastern popular speech, a process that continues to this day. Well-spoken burghers of seventeenth- or eighteenth-century London would be appalled at the number of what they would consider to be newfangled vulgarisms in the pronunciation of Margaret Thatcher or Prince Charles. Present-day General American accents would have a much more familiar ring to them.

John Harris, University College, London WC1.

QUESTION: What are the origins of the expressions 'Cloud nine' and 'Cloud-cuckoo-land'?

☐ 'CLOUD-CUCKOO-LAND' is a translation of the Greek *Nephelokokkugi (Nephele* = cloud, *kokkux* = cuckoo) which is to be found in Aristophanes' comedy, *The Birds*, first performed in 414 BC in Athens. The play concerns two Athenians disillusioned with life in the city who go to seek somewhere better to live. Eventually they conceive to build a city in the air with which they can intercept the sacrificial smoke which nourishes the gods. The birds, under the two Athenians, build the city which is to be called Cloud-cuckoo-land.

John Hudswell, London EC1.

☐ 'CLOUD NINE' is an advance on 'cloud seven', a pictorialisation of the Seventh Heaven (or Heaven of Heaven), the abode of God Himself in both Jewish and Mohammedan tradition; it seems to be an example of the inflationary tendency of the 1960s.

D. W. R. Whicker, Wimborne, Dorset.

QUESTION: As a child in the 1950s I remember reading an hilarious book which began 'I was born in infancy' – and carried on in similar vein. Can anyone tell me the title and author?

☐ THE book was Hermione Gingold's autobiography. It actually began: 'I was born at an early age ...' I forget the title but it was something like *It's a Square World*. I think Hermione Gingold was also the first to use the expression: 'Since I became a virgin ...' and that it was in this book.
Angela Willans, Henley-on-Thames, Oxon.

QUESTION: In the Canadian film, recently shown on television, *I've Heard the Mermaids Singing,* one of the main characters is seen playing a record. The music is an aria which I am trying to trace.

☐ IT IS from the opera *Lakmé* by Delibes. It is a duet from Act I, 'Sous le dôméepais', and is sung by Lakmé and her slave, Mallika. The music is relevant to the film because the 'duettino' expresses the desire of two women to travel along a beautiful stream to its source.
Peter Holloway, Sleaford, Lincs.

QUESTION: Cole and Postgate in their book *The Common People* quote from Charles Kingsley: 'We have used the Bible as if it were a mere special constable's handbook, an opium dose for keeping beasts of burden patient while they are overloaded'. The authors then say 'so sending on its travels a phrase which was to end up on the walls of the Red Square in Moscow in 1917'. They imply that Kingsley influenced Marx in describing religion as an opiate, as he did in his essay, 'Critique of Hegel's Philosophy

of the Right' (1844). So what was the date of the Kingsley quote?

☐ THE passage by Kingsley appeared in the second of the Letters to the Chartists by 'Parson Lot' which was published in the fourth issue of the Christian Socialist paper, *Politics for the People,* on 27 May 1848 – four years after the passage by Karl Marx about religion being 'the opium of the people'.
Nicolas Walter, London N1.

☐ KINGSLEY used the term on more than one occasion and it is not certain when he first used it, but his major theological work was written while he was still a student (completed while a Deacon), and his Christian Socialist period was largely in the first half of the 1840s.

However, his usage was not the earliest recorded (though he may have been unaware of any earlier use of the phrase). A history of the Tory Party in the latter half of the eighteenth century (I forget the author's name but she wrote it about 12 years ago) quotes a Tory MP, speaking in the House of Commons in the 1780s, as having used the phrase. Moreover, she quoted it so casually and with no reference to a startled audience, that one was left to conclude that the saying was already well known then.

However, it should be noted that there is one major difference; Kingsley and the Tory both said 'Opium of the People', Marx said 'Opiate'. The difference is significant. Opium was then a legal drug (in the form of laudanum) commonly used by the upper and upper-middle classes as a self-indulgence. Opiates were used under prescribed medical conditions, for the relief of pain.

Kingsley and the Tory saw religion (in Kingsley's case in the distorted forms of Chiliasm, or Pietism) as the lower class's form of self-indulgence; Marx as ('the heart

of a heartless world') a regrettable necessity for surviving under the prevailing conditions.
Laurens Otter, Wellington, Salop.

QUESTION: Whatever happened to Spangles?

☐ THE Spangle was a last-ditch attempt to revitalise the boiled sweet, which had suffered a grievous loss of credibility among children by being approved of by grandparents.

The fatal blow was inflicted by the proliferation of brands of similarly packaged cough sweets which were regarded by the boiled sweet purchasing classes as even more virtuous than the Spangle as they were not only boring, but tasted vile as well.
Steve Manthorp, Keighley, W. Yorks.

QUESTION: Some years ago I read a book by a Russian dissident, which was called something like *Will the Soviet Union Survive until 1984?* In view of the recent happenings it would be interesting to read it again. Can anyone help with the correct title and author?

☐ THE title was indeed *Will the Soviet Union Survive until 1984?* by Andrei Amalrik, published in this country by Penguin in 1970. The ISBN of this edition is 0713901659.
Mike Innes, Acting County Librarian, Kent County Council, Margate.

QUESTION: Who was the composer of Happy Birthday?

☐ WORDS and music were by an American nursery teacher called Patty Hill. She wrote it so her children could sing it when someone had a birthday.
Chloe Walker (aged 7), Bristol, Avon.

☐ IT IS, I understand, the world's most sung song. Written in the 1890s, it was not copyrighted until 1935 and is still in copyright. In 1988 the firm which had owned the song since 1935 put it up for sale. This company had been collecting about a million dollars a year in royalties. It was acquired by Warner Communications in a $25 million deal.
Leslie Jerman, Epping, Essex.

QUESTION: What happens to spiders washed down the plughole?

☐ THEY drown, naturally. Your reader will no doubt be aware that this barbaric practice was once common in less civilised households. People used to assume that spiders made their way into the bath via the drains (swimming through the U-bend). Of course, we now know that spiders find their way into the bath from above. They then discover that they cannot scale the steep, slippery sides of the bath and remain stuck there until help arrives. The practice of washing spiders down plugholes is, one hopes, a thing of the past. But legend has it that there are still some who spurn the fascinating artistry of a spider in a well-formed web. These households, it is said, can be identified by the clouds of midges and flies that plague them as a result.
Robin Howard, Haywards Heath, W. Sussex.

☐ MINE are strong: they crawl back up again.
Judith Thomas, Wells.

QUESTION: About 25 years ago the *Guardian* carried an article about 'green light' which required virtually no energy. Was this a hoax or was the patent bought out by a light bulb manufacturer?

☐ THE green light is the biochemical reaction used by glow-worms and fireflies to produce a cold light. Synthesis of the natural luciferin and luciferase enzyme has presumably not proved a commercial possibility.
Peter L. G. Bateman, Rentokil Ltd, E. Grinstead, W. Sussex.

☐ I SUSPECT the light was not chemical luminescence, which I believe is available as a rather unsatisfactory emergency light called 'Light Stick', or some such, but electroluminescence. I have a 3in x 2in panel using this principle, bought from Proops Bros in about 1960. It is a grey enamelled steel plate, said to have been sealed with a layer of glass, but still susceptible to moisture, and less than half a millimetre thick. It still works, taking negligible current from 240v AC mains, and running quite cold; it is not a competitor for tungsten bulbs, as the inquirer feared, as it is barely visible in normal room light, although it shines bravely in the dark with a rather bilious blue-green light.
Brooke Harvey, Dunmow, Essex.

QUESTION: The big bang theory deals with the formation of matter, but not with the formation of the space or dimensions into which matter could expand. Does matter create its own space for expansion, or is the Beginning conceived as something like a pea suspended in the Albert Hall with limitlesss, though empty space already in existence for matter to fill?

□ THE big bang theory can deal only with the formation of matter, not the formation of space. Space is an all-pervasive, eternal ultimate, unanalysable into anything simpler or more primitive. Speculation therefore about a 'non-space' prior to a 'formation' of space is meaningless. It is also limitless, certainly unlimited by the walls of the Albert Hall. What could be beyond those walls except more space?
Donald P. Maw, Mansfield, Notts.

□ MANIFEST objective space may be thought of as root matter. At the start of the formation of a cosmos it 'curdles' – or condenses – and eventually tenuous forma-tions become visible, rather as volumes of fog manifest from humid air. As this space is boundless it has no locatable points. This means it has no centre. It also means it only has an edge – or horizon – relative to the observer.

Manifestation, or what the astronomer calls the Origin of the Universe and the priest Creation, is thus a process of condensation, or crystallisation, from all points; and is not an expansion of a highly compressed nucleus through the agency of some explosive force.

But the modern popular myth known as the 'big bang' has lasted as long as it has chiefly because of the very persuasive evidence of the red shift of galactic groups, which is interpreted as recessional speed.

The next revolution in astronomy will come with the general acceptance of the fact that red shift is not indicative of expansion but is a phenomenon caused by the (apparent) near-infinite density of space at any observer's horizon.

Alan Hughes (RIBA), London W5.

QUESTION: Is there a song containing the line: 'When the night goes tremulous'?

☐ THERE is a song by the name of Friend o' Mine, words by Fred E. Weatherby, music by Wilfred Sanderson (1913) which contains the words, 'So, when the night falls tremulous', which was often sung as 'the night grows tremulous'.

D. Holding, Marypool, Cumbria.

QUESTION: What is the origin of the phrase 'to have a chip on one's shoulder'? It sounds American, but where or when?

☐ THIS does seem to be of American origin and derives from a custom once common to bar rooms. A man who felt like a fight put a woodchip on his shoulder and defied anyone to knock it off. The challenge was rarely refused. An Anglo/Irish analogue was (is?) 'trailing the coat'. Here, the would-be gladiator trailed his coat behind him in the hope that someone would tread on it. The formal customs have long ceased but the attitudes remain. Today the allegation that some stranger has merely looked in the wrong direction is deemed sufficient to justify assault. The older usage now seems positively chivalrous.

Alan W. Smith, Chigwell, Essex.

☐ TO ANY North American the origin of the phrase 'a chip on one's shoulder' can be a painful memory. My first experience of it, more than 60 years ago, was as an English child in a Canadian playground. The school bully picked a chip of wood from the ground, placed it on his shoulder, and invited me to knock it off. I did so, and was felled by his fist. In time I learnt that the best method of avoiding an unwanted fight, or the taint of cowardice in refusing the challenge, was to place another chip on my own shoulder and dare my opponent (who was sometimes my friend) to knock that off first. This usually succeeded, and the affair ended painlessly in taunting shouts and honours even.

John Prebble, Kingswood, Surrey.

QUESTION: Why do Jerusalem artichokes produce so much intestinal gas?

☐ THE Jerusalem artichoke, like other roots of the daisy family (e.g. chicory and salsify), contains inulin, a starch composed of fructose (fruit sugar). Human digestive enzymes are produced for starches made from glucose, but many bacteria have more catholic tastes. Undigested inulin arrives in the latter part of the gut and feeds an overgrowth of the intestinal flora, and so produces a noticeable increase in gas output.

The peculiar nature of this starch can be demonstrated by boiling peeled artichokes, with a spoonful of lemon juice and enough water, for an hour or two. This process chops up the inulin chain into its links, providing a high content of very sweet fructose in the resultant syrup.

According to a packet of fructose I read once, this sugar does not promote tooth-rot, so get out there and plant these tuberous sunflowers.
Pat Hemphill, Hulme, Manchester.

QUESTION: Can anyone identify the piece of music used in the Bailey's Irish Cream commercial on TV?

☐ IT IS the Barcarolle from Offenbach's *Tales of Hoffman*.
D. W. Martin, Glasgow.

☐ THE piece is performed beautifully on the LP, *Golden Opera*, by Joan Sutherland and Huguette Tourangeau (Decca 414205-1; 414205-4 cassette).
A. Zalewska, Huddersfield.

QUESTION: We all know that curry dishes originated in the East, but who first used spices in this manner?

☐ THE word 'curry' derives from a Tamil word meaning sauce. Many important spices such as pepper, cardamom and turmeric are indigenous to southern India and India remains the world's largest spice producer.

The art of using blends of spices in the many kinds of Indian cooking has developed over thousands of years. The use of an extensive range of herbs and spices is the unifying factor in various Indian cuisines.

The oldest record of spices in Indian cooking is in the Rig-Veda, dating from around 6000 BC. The epic *Ramayana* of the same period mentions a meat pilaff, containing meat, rice and vegetables cooked with the spices pepper, saffron, mace and raw mango powder.
Hillary Box, Indian Spices Information Bureau, London.

□ THE earliest known reference to the use of spices in cooking can be found in what is considered to be the earliest recipe in existence, made on a clay tablet in the Akkadian language and written in cuneiform script. The tablet is 3,700 years old and is Babylonian in origin.

The reference to curry spices comes in a recipe for braised turnips, which is recorded as an accompaniment to kid stew and tarru-bird stew. The translation of the recipe is as follows: 'Meat is not needed. Boil water. Throw fat in. [Add] onion, dorsal thorn [the name of an unknown plant used as seasoning], coriander, cumin and kanasu [a legume]. Squeeze leek and garlic and spread [juice] on dish. Add onion and mint.'
Tim Thornborough, London SW20.

QUESTION: Why do the media refer to President de Clerk of South Africa as 'President F. W. de Clerk'? They don't refer to 'President G. Bush' or 'President F. Mitterrand'.

□ ALMOST certainly because President de Klerk prefers to be called by his initials, rather than his actual names. His predecessor was similarly known as 'P. W. Botha' (pronounced 'pier fear' in Afrikaans). Many persons of Afrikaans origin are given family Christian names which are often cumbersome and unwieldly. It therefore becomes much easier to refer to people by their initials rather than their names themselves, which if retained, are generally given shortened forms, e.g. Pik Botha. In the case of F. W. these initials are pronounced 'eff fear' in Afrikaans, so are far less of a mouthful than in English.

Another factor is the large number of people sharing certain surnames, and hence the more popular Christian names, so that using the combination of initials reduces the confusion that could otherwise arise.
P. E. Pleming, Cookham Rise, Berks.

QUESTION: Which London park(s) were used by Antonioni for the location shots, especially the 'murder', in his film, *Blow-Up*?

☐ AMAZINGLY, the apparently spacious location was the small Maryon Park at Charlton in south-east London, just off the Woolwich Road. When I visited it soon after the release of the film I found it so hemmed in by council flats I wondered they were never glimpsed by the cameras. A proud park-keeper who identified where the 'murder' had taken place and who took me to the tennis courts that feature in the film gave final proof when he directed me to the men's lavatory used by the film crew and pointed to some neat graffiti – an arrow pointing downwards and the boldly printed legend, 'David Hemmings pissed here.' Maybe by now there's a blue plaque?
Frank Miles, Beckenham, Kent.

☐ THE bushes behind which the body was hidden had been placed there for the film and the group of students miming at the end were from Goldsmith's College.
Mike and Philippa Brandon, Ipswich, Suffolk.

☐ ANTONIONI was living in reduced circumstances in a boarding house on Woolwich Road at the time. He was out walking his dog, Aristotle, one morning, and came upon the park.
Richard Proctor, London SE14.

☐ THE large houses overlooking the park in some shots were actually false, being scenery propped up in the trees at the southern end of the park. David Hemmings's studio/house was on Pottery Lane in Holland Park, adjacent to the Earl of Zetland public house. The site of the antique shop (actually an antique shop only during filming) is in Clevely Close, SE7, opposite one of the entrances to Maryon Park. The shop has been replaced by a more modern general store. I would be keen to converse with others who are also interested in this film.

Graham Armfield, 11 Wolseley Road, Tunbridge Wells, Kent TN4 9BJ.

QUESTION: Does anybody play serious draughts any more? Are there draughts clubs or tournaments? Who is the current champion?

☐ THE English Draughts Association is seven years from its centenary, but we have books and records going back to 1756, and to medieval times, when somewhat different rules applied. The current British champion is 66-year-old Derek Oldbury. Every four years Ireland, Wales, Scotland, England and Guernsey compete in the Home Internationals. Every six years Great Britain and Ireland play the USA.

T. A. Landry, EDA Publicity Officer, 53 Hillfield Road, London NW6 1QD. Tel 071-431 1217.

QUESTION: Can anyone provide the words of the rhyme which enables one to remember English Kings and Queens?

> ☐ WILLIE, Willie, Harry Ste
> Harry, Dick, John, Harry Three,
> One, two, three Neds, Richard Two,
> Henry Fourth, Fifth, Sixth, then who?
> Neddy, Neddy, Dick the Bad,
> Harrys twain and Ned the Lad
> Mary, Bessie, James the Vain,
> Charlie, Charlie, James again,
> William and Mary, Anna Gloria,
> Four Georges, William and Victoria.

Note: More than 130 people sent us the words of the mnemonic (or mnemonarch, as one called it). There were several suggestions as to how it should continue after Victoria:

☐ EDWARD the Seventh next, and then
George the Fifth in 1910.
Edward the Eighth soon abdicated
And so a George was reinstated.
After Lizzie Two (who's still alive)
Comes Charlie Three and Willie Five.
*Richard Fattorini, Bridgend,
Mid-Glamorgan.*

☐ EDWARD, George, then Edward Eight,
George; now Bess is Head of State.
E. L. Isaacs, Barnet, Herts.

☐ THEN came Edward, late in life,
Stiff George and Eddie born to strife,
Gentle George and Lillibet
Good old Charlie, but not just yet.
Freda John, Alvaston, Derby

QUESTION: Had the Duke of Windsor not abdicated and remained King until his death, who would be the sovereign now?

☐ ASSUMING that he married Mrs Simpson and this union produced no children, as was the case, his eldest surviving brother, Henry, Duke of Gloucester, would have become King Henry IX in 1972 at the age of 72. Henry's reign would have lasted only two years before his death in 1974. Of Henry's two sons, the eldest, William, had died in a tragic accident two years before his father's death, thus leaving his brother, Richard Duke of Glouces-

ter, to ascend to the throne as King Richard IV in 1974 and remain as such to the present day.

Having reached his 45th birthday only in 1989, his reign would look set to be one of the longest in our history and certainly more lengthy and agreeable than that of his namesake and only other Duke of Gloucester to reign over us, Richard III.

A. W. Overhead, Wellingborough, Northants.

☐ MR OVERHEAD would, in an earlier time, be in danger of losing his head over the traitorous proposition that an heir to the throne having the misfortune to predecease the sovereign thereby disinherits his own heirs. In 1837 when William IV, the third and eldest surviving son of George III, died childless (or at least without legitimate issue) the crown passed not to the fifth son, Ernest Duke of Cumberland, nor to the sixth son, the Duke of Sussex, nor yet to the seventh son, the Duke of Cambridge, but to the daughter of the predeceased fourth son, the late Duke of

Kent. English history would have been very different with King Ernest I instead of Queen Victoria on the throne.

In the same way, if Edward VIII had not abdicated but had still died childless in 1972, the crown would have gone to the next eldest brother (George, Duke of York), but as he had already died it would not have gone to the next surviving brother (Henry, Duke of Gloucester) but to the Duke of York's daughter, none other than Elizabeth II. Your (and Her Majesty's) loyal servant.
Ian Verber, Richmond, N. Yorks.

Note: our thanks to 76 other readers who wrote to make this point.

☐ IN response to Mr Verber and the 76 other loyalists who would have my traitorous head (or at least confine me to the Tower for usurpatory plotting), I must outline my plan to save my neck. My reference to Richard III was no idle remark. I was actually plotting to gain my own place in history by initiating the Second War of the Roses.

By reading Anne Mortimer for Elizabeth II and Henry Bolingbroke for Richard Duke of Gloucester, any historians among you will realise my cunning plan. The situation that arose during the fifteenth century was remarkably similar to that which would have arisen had the Duke of Windsor not abdicated. Anne Mortimer was the female descendant of the second son of Edward III and Henry Bolingbroke was the male descendant of the third son of Edward III. Although Anne had a stronger claim, she and her family were swept aside by the ambitious Henry and the House of Lancaster. Despite Anne's claim being further strengthened by her marriage to Richard of York (descendant of fourth son of Edward III), her family remained in the shadow of the Lancastrian kings, Henry IV, V and VI, who basked in the glory of the war against France. The House of York then seized their opportunity when Henry VI lapsed into insanity and Anne's son Richard became Lord Protector in 1454.

When Henry regained his sanity the following year, the struggle between the two houses broke out into the War of the Roses.

So it would appear that my coup has been nipped in the bud – and how disturbing it was to realise that the citizen who thwarted my efforts should reside in the county of Yorks. As any fifteenth century opportunist would do, I now align myself with the popular loyalist cause and renounce my earlier allegiances. I bow my head (keeping a wary eye out for the executioner's axe) and also pledge my loyalty to Her Majesty.

A. W. Overhead, Wellingborough, Northants.

QUESTION: Why is it that sunset begins to get later from December 17, while sunrise only gets earlier after January 7 (data in *Whitaker's Almanack*)?

☐ THE problem is one of human making rather than of the physical universe. The earth has a very slightly elliptical orbit and so the days are of slightly different lengths. The time between two solar noons (when the sun is due south) is not precisely 24 hours, and so to divide each day into twenty-fourths would give us 'hours' of changing duration. For his convenience, man has usually kept the length of the day fixed in his reckoning. This is known as Mean Time, as in 'GMT'. The error between Mean Time and Solar Time is as much as 16 minutes in November, and this error is called the Equation of Time.

In December the daylight hours decrease until the 21st and then increase. By Solar Time, sunrise is later until that date and then earlier. We convert Solar Time to Mean Time, but in December the difference, the Equation of Time, is changing fast, and so the time of sunrise in Mean Time does not follow the same pattern as in Solar Time.

Benjamin Fender, Stockbridge, Hants.

QUESTION: Was Bob Dylan using a literary quotation for the title of his song 'All Along the Watchtower'? If so, who was the original poet?

☐ IN the opinion of many analysts of Dylan's work, it refers to the fall of Babylon prophesied in Isaiah 21.

This seems to be confirmed by comparing the opening lines of the song: 'All along the watchtower, princes kept the view' with verse 5 of Isaiah 21 which reads: 'Prepare the table, watch in the watchtower, eat, drink: arise ye princes, and anoint the shield.'

Much of the haunting imagery that Dylan evokes in this short song would appear to owe much to the same text. Namely the two sinister horsemen who approach, both in Dylan's closing lines and in verse 9 of the same chapter.
C. Whitehouse, London SW18.

☐ THIS connection is also suggested in the definitive biography of Dylan, *No Direction Home*, where Robert Shelton quotes a suggestion that the watchtower seems related to the fortified city as a recurring image for the moral state of man or the body politic.
Bernard Tucker, Winchester.

QUESTION: A few years ago I read of a sea waterfall somewhere in the north-west Highlands. Apparently the rock strata slope in such a way as to restrict the drainage of sea water as the tidal level drops. Where and when can this be seen?

☐ THE 'sea waterfall' is probably the Falls of Lora at the mouth of Loch Etive, near Oban. The phenomenon occurs especially at low spring tides.
J. Moreland Craig, Burton-in-Kendal, Cumbria.

QUESTION: Who was Gordon Bennett?

☐ JAMES Gordon Bennett (1841-1918) was an American journalist, editor of the *New York Herald* (in succession to his less well-known father, also James Gordon Bennett) and sports enthusiast. He is probably best-known now for being the man who commissioned Henry Morton Stanley to search for Dr Livingstone (thus presumably occasioning a telegram which began 'Gordon Bennett – I've found Livingstone!'). Bennett also introduced polo to the United States and was involved in horse-racing (Leopold Bloom spends some time in *Ulysses* contemplating a bet upon a horse in the Gordon Bennett Handicap, actually run that day in Dublin).
Nicholas Graham, Teddington, Middx.

☐ IN January 1876 Stanley saw a great mountain 'afar off' and named it Mount Gordon Bennett. This was later changed to the Ruwenzori, better known, perhaps, as the Mountains of the Moon.
Rennie Bere, Bude, Cornwall.

☐ WHEN Bennett opened his newspaper's Paris office in 1887, he was unable to dine at a busy restaurant, so he bought it and sat down to mutton chops.
Paul Crowther, Knutsford, Cheshire.

☐ IN 1900 he donated the Gordon Bennett trophy for a race between national teams of drivers and cars. The complex qualifying process for entry led to the exclamation: Gordon Bennett!
George Hartshorn, Badby, Daventry.

☐ ONCE after a heavy drinking bout at a party arranged by his fiancée, he took advantage of the blazing fire to relieve himself in front of the assembled guests. For which he was thrown out and later horsewhipped by his fiancée's brother with whom he once fought a duel. So as the latest escapade spread among the gossips all shook their

heads in disbelief and despair and said 'Oh, Gordon Bennett!'
Rev. W. Webb, Guildford, Surrey.

☐ MY sister-in-law, a born and bred Eastender, insists that 'Gordon Bennett' is just a politely extended form of 'Gawd', to avoid accusations of blasphemy.
Si Cowe, Pickering, N. Yorks.

QUESTION: Is the leader of an orchestra always a violinist, and if so, why?

☐ THESE days the leader usually will be the principal first violin, except in those rare pieces in the standard repertoire which have no violins, such as the Brahms A major Serenade. In this piece the leader would be the principal viola.

The practice arises from a time when the idea of a conductor directing from the rostrum was yet to be established. A body of players would be directed by either the keyboard player providing the continuo or, when this practice declined in the eighteenth century, from the first violin.
Geoffrey Thomason, Handforth, Cheshire.

QUESTION: It's (almost) officially admitted that MI5 and MI6 exist. During the Second World War there was, I believe, MI9 and MI14. But what did MIs 1-4, 7, 8, 10, 11, 12 and 13 do?

☐ THIS question shouldn't really be asked – or answered – but basically it seems probable they did nothing, but drew pay for it. It is believed that MI1 and MI11 were eliminated long ago because of confusion between Is and 1s in the accounts department.

As to the rest, it is said that out of the huge sums voted as 'contingencies' modest amounts are transferred to MI2 and MI3 and allocated to the Prime Minister and Home Secretary to reward their alleged responsibilities for the non-existing MI5 and MI6. Further amounts, charged to MI4 account, may be offered either to the Chancellor of the Exchequer or to the Foreign Secretary to compensate for loss of tied week-end cottages – and similar.

The large balance (charged to MIs 7, 8, 10, 12 and 13, which are 'notional' only) is used as necessary to bump up 'invisibles' in specially bad months to keep Balance-of-Payment deficits below the £2 billion mark, where possible. But please note, this is off the record.
A. I. Pottinger, Edgbaston, Birmingham.

QUESTION: To, either out of ignorance or boldly and with malice aforethought, insert words into a verb's infinitive form is considered grammatically sinful. Why?

☐ BECAUSE the question has to be read twice to be understood.
Andrew Mackay, London N1.

☐ IN defence of bad syntax, every child should be able to quote the following heroes of twentieth century culture ...

Raymond Chandler wrote to his English publisher: 'When I split an infinitive, god damn it, I split it so it stays split.'

There can be few people who don't know the major contribution of Captain James T. Kirk to the English language ('...our five-year mission – to boldly go where no man has gone before').
Arabella McIntyre Brown, Liverpool 17.

☐ LOST for appropriate models, eighteenth century grammarians turned to Latin when a need was felt to regularise or standardise English. In Latin, of course, it is not possible to split an infinitive – it's one word. Arbitrarily this 'rule' was applied to English.

Bob Jope, Head of English and Drama, Sydenham High School, London SE26.

☐ SHAKESPEARE did it, the *Guardian* regularly does it, and I for one will continue to happily do it without any anxiety over its supposed incorrect or even 'sinful' nature. Of course the rule is to pedantically be observed when, as in this sentence, it leads us into ugliness.

Sean Barker, Moss Side, Manchester.

QUESTION: Can anyone provide me with a recipe for making halva at home?

☐ I FOUND three different recipes in different Greek recipe books. The most successful recipes for Greek dishes are handed down by word of mouth, which explains the variations.

Ingredients: 4oz butter, 1 cup coarse semolina, ½ cup almonds (blanched and slivered), cinnamon. **For syrup:** 1 cup sugar, 1 tablespoon honey, 1½ cups water.

Method: Melt butter in saucepan, add semolina and almonds. Brown, stirring continuously. Remove from heat and add cinnamon. Combine sugar, honey and water in another saucepan. Boil for three minutes, stirring continuously. Blend with semolina mixture and heat for three minutes.

Pour into greased rectangular baking tray and bake for approx. 15 minutes in moderate oven. When cool cut into squares and sprinkle with cinnamon.

Mrs Diana Charalambous, Wallington, Surrey.

QUESTION: Why is the Hundred Foot Drain (New Bedford River) so called? It is neither 100 feet deep nor wide nor long.

☐ I LIVE only a minute or two from it and today measured the present width of the flow which is in excess of 120 feet, although the level is at least six feet below the top of the retaining banks. The questioner must have seen it only in summer, not when it is called upon to perform its job of carrying off the excess water of the Great Ouse.
D. C. Bennett, Huntingdon, Cambs.

QUESTION: Can anyone give me the words, normally sung chorally, to *Finlandia* by Jean Sibelius?

☐ ANY poem/hymn in 10, 10, 10, 10, 10, 10 or 11, 10, 11, 10 metre will fit the tune. The two most common poems are that by Harriet Beecher Stowe – 'Still, still with Thee' or that by J. Quarles and H. F. Lyte beginning 'Long did I toil'. There is also a poem by Katharina von Schlegel – 'Be still my soul'.

Most hymn books now have one or other versions of these, but often to other tunes.
R. G. Daniels, Northampton.

☐ THESE are the words sung to *Finlandia* at the annual 'international' evening of the Lancashire Federation of Women's Institutes. They are very moving:

> This is my song, O God of all the Nations,
> A song for peace for lands afar and mine,
> This is my love, the country where my heart is,
> This is my hope, my dream, my shrine,
> But other hearts in other lands are beating,
> With other dreams, the same as mine.

(Mrs) Mary Highfield, Barton,
nr Preston, Lancs.

QUESTION: How did the newt, a graceful and agile creature, come to be regarded as an index of inebriation?

☐ IT WAS a mistake, a mishearing of 'an Ute', as used by US Army personnel in Britain during the Second World War. The celebrated drunkenness of the Ute Indian tribe on their reservation forced the US Government to ban the sale of alcohol there.
Harold Smith, Bradford-on-Avon, Wilts.

☐ THE phrase actually comes down to regional accent in the days of Henry VIII. Half-way through a banquet the king inquired as to what brew one young reveller had been partaking of, to be begged by the young man's father to 'forgive him, Sire, he is but a youth and as for wine he is new to it!' Hence he was p_ _ _ _ _ as a 'new to it'.
Lesley Robertson, London SW4.

☐ NEWTS, like many other small creatures which were easily found in the countryside around places where beer was being brewed or cider pressed, were often added to the barrels of drink to improve flavour and strength.

An article in *Tenth-Century Studies* by David Parsons remarks that the medieval practice was to put mice or weasels in beer to flavour it, but it was considered sinful to do this deliberately and cruelly drown the beasts, so the English got the priest to bless the beer first. This absolved them, since the animals were going into a holy liquid.

Cider-makers in Somerset have been known to add lumps of beef to the fermenting juice, and stories circulate about rats floating in barrels of scrumpy.

The newt as an amphibian would survive in liquid longer than mouse, weasel and rat, and presumably would pass so much alcohol through its gills that it would soon reach that happy state wherein its grosser bodily functions would be a matter of complete indifference to it.
Angela Costen, Axbridge, Somerset.

☐ AMAZED that three people could supply different but equally mistaken answers, we feel it our duty to provide the correct answer. Abraham Newton (1631-1698) of Grantham, the presumed author of the first known treatise on the medicinal properties of the beer of Burton-upon-Trent (now unfortunately lost), was such a well-known tippler that, in his lifetime, even Londoners would use the expression 'Pissed as Abe Newton.' He was so famous that when his fellow townsman, Isaac Newton, achieved prominence, people would say of him, 'No, not that Newton.' The confusion reached its height in the early 1700s, so it was probably around this time that 'pissed as a Newton' sprang into being, only to be gradually contracted into the phrase we all know so well.
M. and B. Gidley, Exeter.

QUESTION: Alfred Hitchcock reputedly appears briefly in all his films, but where can I find him in *Psycho*?

☐ EXACTLY 6 minutes, 13 seconds into the film (this includes the opening credits), the director can be glimpsed standing outside the bank (wearing a stetson hat) just as Janet Leigh is entering.
Nigel Parkin and Andrew Willis, Nottingham.

☐ HITCHCOCK appears as one of a group of pedestrians on a road crossing who pass in front of Janet Leigh's car. She is leaving town after stealing from her employer and in fact is recognised as a result of having stopped at the crossing.
Susan Carey, Hayling Island, Hants.

☐ HIS ritual appearances (usually as a passer-by) are listed in an extended interview with François Truffaut. He tells Truffaut about the trouble he had finding a role for himself in *Lifeboat* because you can't have a passer-by

on the ocean. He thought he might play a dead body floating past in the sea, but ruled it out in case he sank. In the end he had William Bendix open an old newspaper to reveal the familiar outline in an advert for a mythical slimming drug, Reduco – an idea inspired by a diet that Hitchcock was on at the time. His 'before' and 'after' photos in the spoof ad were so impressive, claimed Hitch, that he was besieged by enquiries from fat people eager to find out where they could buy Reduco.
John Sibbald, Whitley Bay, Tyne and Wear.

☐ HIS cameos were usually in the opening minutes of the film so as not to distract the audience from following the plot by looking for his appearance.
Ben Francis, Liverpool 17.

QUESTION: Who allocates names to hurricanes?

☐ THE US Weather Bureau allocates names on a five-year cycle, alternating male and female names from A to W. However, other countries may give their own names. The practice was first described in George Stewart's 1941 novel, *Storm*, and seems to have become commonplace, although unofficial, before the end of the Second World War.

Weather Bureau allocations began in 1953, and until 1979 only girls' names were used, but since then both sexes have been represented. Names given to particularly memorable storms have to be 'retired', and there is a shortage of appellations for the early part of the alphabet, hence the need to use the likes of 'Alicia', 'Chantal' and 'Dean'.

Research shows that people identify much more closely with a named storm, and are far more willing to evacuate low-lying coasts as he/she approaches.
Bill Carter, Coleraine, N. Ireland.

QUESTION: My television licence states that if I wish to use a video recorder with a black-and-white TV it is necessary to obtain a colour TV licence. Why?

☐ THE law requires that any apparatus receiving colour transmissions has to have a colour licence. A video recorder has a colour 'discriminator', as does a colour television set, and a video recorder records colour signals. *Bob Devine, Deputy Field Operations Manager, TV Licensing Organisation, Bristol.*

QUESTION: I believe that it is possible to avoid junk mail by writing to an organisation that will remove your name from mailing lists. Do any readers know of such an organisation?

☐ THERE are two addresses that one can write to to prevent junk mail being delivered. They are: Mailing

Preference Service, Freepost 22, London W1E and Office of the Data Protection Registrar, Springfield House, Water Lane, Wilmslow SK9 5AX. If you write to these two bodies they will remove your name from the computerised mailing lists.
Mark Peters, c/o Royal Mail Letters, Harrow, Middx.

☐ THE Mailing Preference Society can only control mailings from organisations affiliated to the scheme, and addressed to you personally at home (i. e. items addressed to 'the occupier' or 'householder' are outside its scope). Additionally, you can use the scheme to receive more unsolicited mailings should you feel you are not getting a sufficient supply of 'Win a Car'/'Your Lucky Number Is ...' type correspondence.
Barry Mills, London SE6.

QUESTION: Why do we say *Oxford* Street (stress on the Oxford), but Oxford *Road* (stress on the road)?

☐ YOU can't always expect language to be logical. There are two principles in conflict here. One is the general rule of giving noun-plus-noun compounds early stress, as in BEAUTy contest, MUSic lesson. The other is the more restricted rule of putting late stress on phrase-like compounds where the first element refers to a location, as in kitchen WINDow, Camden TOWN. In fact 'street' is the only thoroughfare-word which follows the first pattern: all the others (Oxford AVenue, Oxford CIRCus, Oxford CRESCent) are like Oxford ROAD. There is a similar inconsistency in our saying CHRISTmas cake but Christmas PUDDing, and ORange juice but orange SQUASH.

Other cases involve a difference of meaning, as when we compare a TOY factory (for manufacturing toys) with a toy FACTory (for a child to play with), or a MOVing van (pantechnicon) with a moving Van (not stationary). The stress patterns of compounds and phrases are extensively documented in my *Longman Pronunciation Dictionary*, published recently.

J. C. Wells, Professor of Phonetics, University College, London.

QUESTION: What are the fumes given off by photocopiers? Are they harmful?

☐ THE pungent-smelling fumes (also given off by laser printers) are ozone, the unstable form of oxygen produced when a high-energy electrical discharge passes through air and rearranges the oxygen molecules. The same phenomenon occurs in thunderstorms as a result of lightning bolts.

How harmful ozone is depends on where it is. In the upper atmosphere it is entirely beneficial, as we are all now aware. At nose level it is highly toxic and these machines, useful though they are, should be kept in a well-ventilated position.

David Spry, London W11.

☐ THE principal emission of the photocopying process, Xerography, is ozone. On a regular basis Rank Xerox would receive requests from concerned Health and Safety officers seeking assurance that these emissions were within safe limits. The minute quantity of ozone produced is of no danger to health. Interestingly, we receive far fewer requests in these times of concern about the decline of the world's ozone.

Ted Stockton, Rank Xerox, Manchester.

☐ IN a guidance note from the Health and Safety Executive, 1976, the threshold limit value (short-term exposure limit) for ozone is given as 0.3 parts per million.

Considering that the smell of ozone is apparent in quantities as little as one part per 500,000, it seems that if

one can smell the fumes, according to the HSE, safety guidelines are being contravened.
Peter Finan, Eccleshill, Bradford.

QUESTION: What did William Blake have in mind when he used the expression 'dark satanic mills'?

☐ THE phrase was used in the preface to *Milton* (1804) and refers not to the new cotton mills or factories but, as David Erdman suggests (*Blake: Prophet Against Empire* [3rd edn, 1977], p.396), to the 'mills that produce dark metal, iron and steel, for diabolic purposes'. At the time London was 'a major war arsenal and the hub of the machinery of war' – the war against the French had been renewed in 1803 after a brief peace – and Blake's symbolism was part of what Erdman calls Blake's 'determination to forge counterarms of art' (p.395).
Keith McClelland, London N4.

QUESTION: Why is Portsmouth called Pompey?

☐ A LADY, known throughout the navy as Aggie Weston, ran a hostel and club for sailors at Portsmouth. She used to give talks to them and attracted a large audience to the Sailors' Rest.

It is said that in 1904 she gave a talk on the Roman general, Pompey the Great. She got very worked up about the reasons for his downfall, and when she told of his assassination one of the sailors called out: 'Poor old Pompey!'

A few days later Portsmouth Football Club had a match at Fratton Park. They played badly, and when eventually the inevitable goal was scored against them a sailor in the crowd called out: 'Poor old Pompey!' Others took up the chorus. It became the good-tempered theme for the football terraces and soon attached itself to the town.

Reg Sanders, Alresford, Hants.

QUESTION: Why are there no jockeys in the Jockey Club?

□ WHEN the Jockey Club was founded in the middle of the eighteenth century, 'jockey' still denoted an owner of horses as much as a rider. The club was a social and sporting organisation of wealthy racing men, themselves breeders and amateur riders. The term 'jockey' has only subsequently come to mean a professional rider.

Two examples of ex-jockeys who have been allowed to join are Sir Gordon Richards and Bruce Hobbs; having retired from race-riding, each took up training, and on their retirements from the latter career became members of the Jockey Club. Other ex-jockeys have followed them.

Jess Carrington, E. Dereham, Norfolk.

QUESTION: What is the origin of the expression 'The man on the Clapham omnibus'?

□ THE man makes his debut in the decision of Lord Justice Greer in the 1932 case of Hall vs Brooklands Auto-Racing Club. He appears as that ubiquitous, and mythical, 'reasonable man' in order to set 'reasonable' standards.

In the case itself he is a spectator at a motor racing event where a number of the watching crowd are seriously injured when a car careers through the barrier. To the question of whether the race organisers owed a duty of care to the victims he is made to reply with a firm negative, since 'he would know quite well' that no barrier would provide protection from this 'possible but highly improbable' occurrence. Thus the reasonable man denies any right of compensation.

It might be of interest to know that the 'man on the Clapham omnibus' makes an earlier appearance in the United States as 'the man who takes the magazines home, and in the evening pushes the lawnmower in his shirt sleeves'. Which magazines? One wonders.
Steve Silvester, Garstang, Lancs.

☐ WHILE I do not doubt that Lord Justice Greer referred to the Man on the Clapham Omnibus in his case of 1932, the fact is that he would have been referring to precedent. The first record of the man in question goes back to Lord Bowen in a case dated 1903.
Eric Ogden, Cheadle Hulme, Cheshire.

☐ THE expression is generally attributed to John Burns (1858-1943), the Liberal MP and Cabinet Minister, a working-class Londoner by birth, the man credited with the description of the Thames as 'liquid history'.
Francis Jones, London W5.

☐ IN the *Journal of the Society of Arts* (May 1857), the following passage appears: 'So thoroughly has the tedious traffic of the streets become ground into the true Londoner's nature, that ... your dog-collared occupant of the knife-board of a Clapham omnibus will stick on London Bridge for half-an-hour with scarcely a murmur.' How times don't change!
James W. Thirsk, Hadlow, Kent.

QUESTION: Has anyone heard of a children's book called *The Ticklish Tiger and Other Stories?*

☐ THE Ticklish Tiger, I'm here to relate / Is only one tale in the book (there are eight). / The stories are told in rhythm and rhyme / And to read them aloud takes next to no time. / The Baron de Bong and his nephew and niece, / With the dog-from-next-door and the chief of police, / In utility print had adventures galore, / With humour appealing to children post-war. / My very own copy is crumpled with age / And, sad to relate, I have lost the front page. / 'A Bong Book,' it's labelled, by Brian Grimshaw / Does anyone publish these books any more? *(Mrs) Sandy Collison, Richmond, Surrey.*

QUESTION: When cats are angry they wag their tails, but dogs wag their tails when they are happy. Please explain.

☐ IN all animals the tail is an extension of the spinal column and probably serves to communicate a wide range of signals. Cats can also communicate 'pleasure' by wagging their tails very slowly, but it is wrong to attempt to express animal behaviour in human terms. The dog's tail-wagging may be a mixture of things: not only pleasure but an indication of his relationship with his human friends, his 'status'.

Dogs' behaviour is probably a throwback to their pack origins and their status within it. Hence the ease with which dogs may be trained to be obedient and even subservient to human beings.

Cats are essentially hunters and loners. They have no respect for authority and, as much of their behaviour relates to the need to observe quietly and stalk their prey, a silent means of communication/expression of feelings is an important part of their equipment. Hence, the cat's tail probably has a much greater vocabulary than the dog's, and it may be that in the communication of basic information and emotions the cat's tail is the most important part of its body.
Robert Turpin, Plymouth.

QUESTION: When the Romans built roads in England, they ran in practically straight lines between strategic locations many miles apart. How did they know, if starting in London, which direction to point in to build a straight road to, say, Dover?

☐ BY not starting in London, or at Dover. By finding some high point in the middle and looking both ways.

The middle and main part of this itinerary is the remarkably direct route between Greenwich Park and Canterbury. On the high ground northwest of the Medway crossing there are a few points, e.g. Telegraph Hill and Shorne Ridgeway, where one can see both Shooters Hill, which overlooks Greenwich, and Dunkirk Hill, which overlooks Canterbury.

In essence, there is a fore-and-aft line-up with a definable direction. This overall bearing is not discernible from anywhere on the road itself, yet it is the master bearing of Watling Street Greenwich to Canterbury,

Greenwich Park to Stonewood Pass, and two other main courses east of the Medway – and the referee of all the rest. This is typical of Roman route articulation.

As standard practice, Roman highway engineers converted a sighting offered by nature into a formal bearing and transferred that, or calculated balancing variants thereof, to places of useful application, generally lower down, and sometimes at a considerable remove.

Alec McColm, Upper Bourne End, Bucks.

☐ ALEC McColm's explanation might apply to the Roman road between London and Dover, but it would not explain the remarkable sense of direction which the Romans seemed to show when much greater distances were involved. How did they know, for instance, that they had to strike out north-west from London to get to Chester? Watling Street, although it proceeds in a series of shallow zig-zags, is never very far from the direct line between those two towns. A similar precision is shown by the Fosse Way, which lies on an almost dead straight line from Ilchester in Somerset to Leicester.

Ian Freeman, Ravensden, Bedford.

☐ THE problem about very long Roman roads can be solved if you imagine that you are a Roman surveyor and consider what you have to hand – lots of legionaries, flags which are simple to manufacture, plenty of wood for beacons or fires to make smoke signals. Flags, trumpets and smoke codes pass messages between outposts having line of sight.

When the legions invaded Britain they would have followed the routes taken by the British, using local guides. Many years later when they came to build roads they would have known the rough layout of the countryside.

The method of straightening a known route is not difficult. Send a squad on to each ridge along the route and raise a flag wherever they are. If a squad cannot see the flags on each side, send out another squad. Tell each squad to march along the ridge, until they are directly between the flags of the squads on each side of them, as explained by Alec McColm (see above). Move the flags to the new squad positions. Report problems such as fords, marshes, etc, to the surveyor by flags, trumpet or smoke signals, and receive his instructions.

Repeat this as often as necessary. If there is hilly ground between two mountains, repeat the whole process, using the established positions on the mountains as end points, until all parts of the road can see a flag.

On flat ground smoke from fires would show up better than flags. The whole process would take only a few weeks, or at most a summer season.

(Dr) Dave Fawthrop, Bradford.

□ THE Romans built on the paths created since prehistoric times. These paths, latterly endowed with magical properties by some rather fanciful thinkers, were laid down by surveyors using sighting poles. Many of these were surveyed by Alfred Watkins in 1920 and recorded in his book, *The Old Straight Track*, published in 1925. The early creators of the paths realised the need for good, planned communications, unlike the present Government.

John Garratt, Amersham, Bucks.

□ THE Romans left us miles of roads but not a word as to their surveying and building them. The 'explanations' you have printed cannot account for the fact that a line drawn on a map from Lindum (Lincoln) through Ratae (Leicester) and continued, goes straight to Aquae Sulis (Bath) and Lindinis (Ilchester) and beyond. Furthermore, the length from Lindum to Lindinis is the base of an isosceles triangle with its apex on Londinium. This line is that of the Fosse and the road deviates from it only very slightly.

Peter Ecker, Breston, Derby.

QUESTION: My wife maintains that the final two pages of *The House at Pooh Corner* by A. A. Milne comprise the most poignant passage in English literature. Can anyone suggest alternative candidates for this title?

☐ THE last page in Charles Dickens' *A Tale of Two Cities*: 'It is a far far better thing that I do ...'
(Miss) Lucinda Powell, London W6.

☐ THE last page of *Wuthering Heights*: 'I lingered around them ...'
Diana Johns, King Langley, Herts.

☐ I CAN strongly recommend *Where's Master?* by Caesar, the King's Dog. Caesar belonged to Edward VII and walked immediately behind the gun-carriage at the King's funeral on 20 May, 1910. Hodder & Stoughton published the book on 13 June that year and it reached its ninth edition on 30 August.

Having bought a copy at a book fair, I made the mistake of reading it on the train back. Quite what the other passengers made of an unshaven 35-year-old snivelling over a second-hand book, I am unable to say, but I wish I'd had a handkerchief on me.
John Whiteley, Altrincham, Cheshire.

☐ THE most poignant passage in English (or, perhaps, any other language) is surely the last two pages of *Watership Down*, particularly the third-from-last paragraph, which contains this sentence: 'It seemed to Hazel that he would not be needing his body any more, so he left it lying on the edge of the ditch, but stopped for a moment to watch his rabbits and to try to get used to the extraordinary feeling that strength and speed were flowing inexhaustibly out of him and into their sleek young bodies

and healthy senses.'
   Never fails to make me sniffle.
C. Sullivan, East Dulwich, London.

☐ I NOMINATE 'The Piper at the Gates of Dawn' chapter from *The Wind in the Willows* by Kenneth Grahame. Regrettably, some editions omit this chapter as irrelevant to the plot, so if buying a copy make sure it is unabridged.
Pete Clinch, Dundee.

☐ THE part of the prologue to Evelyn Waugh's *Brideshead Revisited* where Charles Ryder compares his feelings to the Army to that of a husband caught in a failed marriage.
Gillian Kempster, Chobham, Surrey.

☐ AT THE end of Malory's *Morte D'Arthur*, after 20-and-a-half books of cartoon fighting, knights bashing each other about, and it all being jolly fun, the mortally wounded Arthur lies in a chapel near the field of the last battle, and hears cries and shrieks from the field. He sends Sir Lucan to investigate and Lucan sees 'pillours and robbers' picking their way among the dying men on the field, looting from them, killing them for their jewels if they're still alive. Real life has arrived after the golden age of Arthur.
Ian Lewis, Farnham, Surrey.

☐ SURELY the final paragraph of Emily Brontë's *Wuthering Heights*, by many a tear.
Hilary Cripps, Worthing, W. Sussex.

☐ WHETHER at school, in the army, earning a living or now, 70 years on, the pith of poignancy was ever exemplified for me by the words of Charles Lamb: 'I have had playmates, I have had companions, in the days of childhood, in my joyful school-days. All, all are gone, the old familiar faces.'
Frank Carpenter, N. Walsham, Norfolk.

□ THOMAS Hardy is surely the master of poignancy. My choice would be the final three paragraphs of *The Woodlanders* (but read the rest of the book first!)
Andrew Foster, Wickford, Essex.

QUESTION: Why are the police referred to as 'the Bill' or 'the Old Bill'?

□ THE 'Old Bill' seems to be a piece of word play combining the Old Bailey where you went for the more serious offences, with the sought-after Bill Bailey of the popular song. The TV series, *The Bill,* circulated the shorter phrase among those lacking the proper cultural background.
A. W. Smith, Chigwell, Essex.

□ NOTHING to do with Bill Bailey/Old Bailey. Old Bill pre-dates Robert Peel's peelers to the days of the Townman or Watchman – 'Three o'clock and all's well' – who patrolled the night streets of London carrying a lantern and a halberd. The halberd, a long-shafted axe with a hook on the back of the blade, was an early army weapon from the fifteenth century which later became the symbol of authority and denoted the rank of sergeant.

Ex-army halberds were handed on to the Townmen to impart an appearance of officialdom. As usual with army issue, the halberd had a nickname in the ranks: the bill.

The cockneys of the time, to show their derision and lack of respect for the Townmen, and also to let it be known that the Townman's symbol of authority was in fact nothing more than a bit of second-hand army surplus, called the Townman 'Old Bill'.
Red Daniells, London SW2.

QUESTION: Why are dusters yellow?

☐ As an office and industrial cleaner for many years, I offer these suggestions: one of the duster's great attributes is its use for polishing. In the past, before the advent of pressurised canisters and the dreaded CFCs, this was done with beeswax. The manufacturers of such may have decided to make and sell its necessary accompaniment dusters. Wishing to keep an identification with their main product they would naturally have dyed them yellow. Early dusters were not the bright ones of today, but a more ochre colour – indeed, some were pastel green.

Alternatively: an enterprising marketing director of yesteryear may have attempted to corner the market by using most people's association of the colour yellow with springtime, through an increase in sunshine and daylight hours. He would have realised that sales of dusters would be increased enormously by using the appropriate colour especially during the annual spring cleaning season.

There are many examples of how the colour has become connected with spring, such as daffodils and the expression 'to be as busy as a (yellow) bee'. Spring cleaning with (yellow) wax and duster is an almost symbolic gesture of spreading sunlight around the home. *P. Millard, Bristol, Avon.*

☐ If, as P. Millard suggests, dusters were originally coloured yellow in order to work upon the public's association of the colour with the season of spring, then the ploy will probably have been unsuccessful. Despite the increase in sunshine hours and various other yellow connotations, green and not yellow has been shown to be more commonly linked with this particular season.

This was proved by the psychologist, P. H. K. Seymour, in 1976. In order to test a phenomenon of perceptual confusion known as the Stroop effect, Seymour's version of the phenomenon involved the linking of seasons and colours. In order to lay the groundwork for such an experiment, extensive testing found that the majority of people link yellow with summer, brown with autumn, white with winter, and green with spring.

So if, in a few months' time, you find yourself automatically reaching for some green dusters, beware the mind-games played by *Guardian*-reading marketing directors.
Michael A. Martin, London SW20.

☐ I HAVE despaired of reading a sensible explanation for why dusters are yellow. Here is my theory instead. In the first half of the nineteenth century a large quantity of bright yellow cotton cloth was imported from Nanking in China, and subsequently imitated and produced in Britain, from which highly fashionable trousers (Nankeens) were made. After the garments wore out, the remaining cloth was recycled as polishing rag in the hands of the thrifty. Yellow buckskin breeches had been fashionable earlier and they were made of leather, cotton or wool. White linen and cotton rag was usually recycled for high quality paper, and there was never enough.

I do not know if two sense of 'buff', that is (1) yellow ox-leather and (2) to polish with a piece of the same, have anything to do with the matter, but see OED. The traditional association between a yellow material and polishing may have reinforced the use of Nankeen cloth for dusting and cleaning after the fashion for the trousers ceased.
Charles Newton, London N22.

QUESTION: Are floppy disks corrupted by being placed near the floor on tube trains?

☐ IT IS difficult to give a definitive answer. By the very nature of the drive equipment on Underground trains, there is a 'noisy' electromagnetic environment within carriages, although this varies according to the type of train, one's position within the carriage and whether the train is accelerating or braking. It is also true that the susceptibility of disks to corruption varies.

While we can offer no categoric guarantee that disks will not be corrupted, readers may be reassured to know that our own staff have never reported any such problems when transporting disks, nor has our Track Recording Vehicle ever suffered any corruption of data on its own sophisticated computer equipment.

David Bertram, Public Affairs Manager, London Underground, London SW1.

☐ I HAVE had disks damaged in the past and I suspect that a tube ride was the cause. Now, whenever I have to transport floppy disks, I always take two copies and enclose both in a small steel box in my briefcase.

Richard Spence, Lutterworth, Leics.

☐ DURING the trials of the prototype trains for London Underground's Central Line replacement, tests were carried out to determine the magnetic field strength inside the coaches. Although the main concern was the effect on people with heart pace-makers, one of the tests involved placing floppy disks on the carriage floor at the points of highest magnetic field. No corruption of the disks was found.

I am not aware of any similar trials on the older rolling stock, but as these trains contain fewer magnetic field sources there is unlikely to be any adverse effect. Modern electric locomotives generate very high magnetic fields inside (which can have disastrous effects on wrist-watches and cash cards), but these are screened by the steel body. Even in the cab the magnetic field levels are safe, so there would be no effect on a passenger sitting several metres away (inside another steel box).

A more likely cause of a portable computer 'crashing' would be arcing from the pantograph (or shoegear on

Network South-East). This causes electromagnetic impulses similar to lightning.

J. A. Moreland, Withington, Manchester.

☐ THE BBC Micro Live programme once tried in numerous ways to corrupt floppy disks, e.g. by taking them on the tube, leaving them in hot sunlight, putting them under telephones, etc. Of all the possible methods tried, only putting them under a ringing telephone (of the bell rather than warbling type) caused any loss of data. I regularly carry disks on the tube in the course of my work and have never had any problems. I do know of people, however, who use the fact that they are carrying floppy disks or magnetic tapes as a way of getting a taxi fare out of our accounts section, rather than the 70p needed for the tube.

C. Quinn, Huyton, Merseyside.

QUESTION: Does anyone ever win a whopping dirty great big prize after returning lucky numbers in a 'No' envelope?

☐ IF ANYTHING upwards of £60,000 is a 'whopping' prize, then I can certainly confirm that as far as *Reader's Digest* prize draws are concerned, people responding in 'No' envelopes can, and frequently do, win our major prizes.

Tan Mackay, Reader's Digest, London W1.

☐ I CAN answer only for the Consumers' Association, but in our case the answer is definitely 'Yes'. In the period 1985 to 1989, three of the winners in our prize draw competition have been people who didn't want to take up a trial offer of one of our publications against two of the winners who did. The 'No's' won a total of £310,000.

Val Bethell, Head of Press Relations, Consumers' Association, London NW1.

QUESTION: Is there still such a thing as a flea circus?

☐ I EXPECT many readers will have much more up-to-date information, but I did visit and enjoy a flea circus at the Tivoli Gardens, Copenhagen, in 1964.
E. Mautner, London NW11.

☐ TO THE best of my knowledge the last British flea circus was scratched in 1974. Human fleas are now rare within houses and those seeking them will probably only find them on pigs. In contrast, the cat flea is increasing by leaps and bounds but presumably is now protected by some well-meaning Flea Protection Society from performing in public.
P. L. G. Bateman, Director of Public Relations, Rentokil Environmental Services Division, E. Grinstead, W. Sussex.

QUESTION: I have seen labyrinth designs in Chartres cathedral and the Mappa Mundi. But where did this pattern occur before the thirteenth century?

☐ THE labyrinth has an ancient pedigree and some European rock-cut carvings are believed to date from the neolithic age, perhaps about 4,000 years ago. Two fine examples can be seen carved on a rock face at Rocky Valley near Tintagel and are dated to the Bronze Age, about 1500 BC. The Romans made use of the design, especially in their mosaic pavements, and examples are to be found in the museums of Caerleon and Kingston-upon-Hull.

Turf labyrinths, or Troy Towns, were once common in Britain, but only a handful are now in existence, that at Saffron Walden being the largest and best preserved. It is likely that these pre-date ecclesiastical versions, but how old they are is difficult to determine. The labyrinth-dance, or crane-dance, was performed in ancient Greece,

Labyrinth design copied from Chartres Cathedral

following the tortuous twistings of the maze, and no doubt some form of dance once took place within British turf-cut mazes.

Other types of labyrinth exist, including those made from stones, such as at St Agnes in the Scilly Isles, and the huge, enigmatic, three-dimensional maze of Glastonbury Tor, which may be Celtic, or even older.

Those found in cathedrals such as Chartres or Rheims were a Christianisation of a pagan concept and symbolic games and 'pilgrimages' took place along their paths. It is likely that the pagan symbolism involved ideas concerning the inner journey of the individual and soul through the cycle of life, death and rebirth.
Eric Fitch, Burnham, Bucks.

☐ EXAMPLES in various mediums are to be found as far apart as Arizona and Sumatra, as well as here in the UK.

Caerdroia, a research group dedicated to the study of mazes and labyrinths, produces a regular journal and other publications. For details send an SAE.
Jeff Saward, Caerdroia, 53 Thundersley, Benfleet, Essex SS7 3EB.

QUESTION: In Al Pacino's film, *Cruising*, there occurs several times a short piece of baroque instrumental music. Can anyone identify it?

☐ THE music is from *La Musica Notturna di Madrid* (1780) by Boccherini. I've got it on a Deutsche Grammophon compilation called *Adazio*, catalogue no. 2530 247, recorded in 1973.
J. R. Smales, Tottenham, London N17.

QUESTION: I was once informed that a pinball world championship was to be held in London. Where and when?

☐ IT WAS held last year at the Royal Horticultural Halls, Westminster. I won the competition, with a score of around 4.7 million on my second game.

Pinball competitions are also held within the Pinball Owners' Association. There is a monthly contest in Surrey, and an annual convention where the Pinball Wizard is decided. For details drop a line to PO Box 2, Haslemere, Surrey, GU27 2EQ. The club also caters for people interested in old slot-machines and juke boxes. Membership is £8.50 for those resident in the UK, including an excellent magazine.
James Waters, Chadwell Heath, Essex.

QUESTION: Can any of your readers recommend a source of hard-wearing, non-leather boots? I know I am not the only vegetarian who has trouble finding suitable footwear.

☐ I WOULD suggest the 'Bridgedale dry boot' which can be found in most country clothing shops. It is a fairly heavy rubber boot, handmade in Malaysia and of the best quality. I have been wearing a pair for three years now on the roughest part of the North York Moors. They grip very well on the slippery rocks and cope remarkably well with the long and bouncy heather.

They cost only about £33 compared to leather boots that range from £40 to well into the hundreds.
Lawrence Brennan, York.

☐ DOLOMITE, distributed in the UK by MOAC, have been making polyurethane boots for many years, and have just launched two new models, the Ranger and Trekker.

However, the decision not to wear animal skin does seem to be rather at odds with environmental considerations, particularly as most alternatives are made from non-renewable petroleum products.
Christian Leigh, St Albans, Herts.

QUESTION: Has anyone published a line count of Shakespearean roles? What are the top 10?

☐ A LIST of the 20 longest Shakespearean roles was published in 1980, in *The Book of Lists 2*, edited by David Wallechinsky, Irving Wallace, Amy Wallace and Sylvia Wallace. The top ten roles are: 1 Hamlet, 1,422 lines (*Hamlet*); 2 Falstaff, 1,178 (*Henry IV*, parts one and two); 3 Richard III, 1,124 (*Richard III*); 4 Iago, 1,097 (*Othello*); 5 Henry V, 1,025 (*Henry V*); 6 Othello, 860 (*Othello*); 7 Vincentio, 820 (*Measure for Measure*); 8 Coriolanus, 809 (*Coriolanus*); 9 Timon, 795 (*Timon of Athens*); 10 Antony, 766 (*Antony and Cleopatra*).

However, Falstaff would top the list (with 1,614 lines) if his 436 lines in *The Merry Wives of Windsor* are included. Now, if we permit this, then it seems to me that Henry V must be allowed his lines from *Henry IV*, as

Prince Henry. He would have (by my count) a further 117 lines, giving him a total of 1,142 lines and third place.
Brian Smith, Harrow, Middx.

QUESTION: If a plane flies because of the lift from its wing-shape (cross-section), how can a plane fly upside-down, where this same 'lift' would draw it to the ground?

☐ WHEN an aircraft moves forward through the air, its wings deflect the air downwards. It is the reaction to this force on the air that lifts the plane up. The shape of the cross-section of the wing is important, but the main requirement is that the wing should be at an angle to the flow of air past it, such that its leading edge is higher than its trailing edge. The pilot controls this angle by varying the lift on the tailplane by raising and lowering the elevator.

If an inverted wing has its leading edge lower than its trailing edge, it will indeed give negative lift. An example is the 'wings' fitted to racing cars, which push the wheels down on to the road. When an aircraft loops the loop, negative lift is required at the top of the loop to aid gravity in supplying the necessary centripetal force.

The wings on an aircraft are set on the fuselage so that they have a positive 'angle of attack' with the fuselage level. For straight and level inverted flight, this built-in angle of attack has to be cancelled, and an angle of attack in the opposite sense applied as the leading edge has to be higher than the trailing edge. This involves the plane adopting a very tail-down attitude when inverted. Thus inverted flight is possible, but very inefficient.
Jim Stacey, Thornton, Liverpool 23.

QUESTION: Why does the Latin mass contain a Greek Kyrie Eleison?

☐ THE Kyrie is all that remains of a litany which once invariably preceded the Eucharistic Liturgy (and still does in some rites). It first appeared in the Greek Orient in the fourth century.

Before the Bishop recites a prayer, a series of biddings is announced by the deacon to which all respond 'Kyrie Eleison'. The practice was probably introduced to the West by pilgrims returning from the Holy Land. In some liturgies the reponse was translated into Latin, but at Rome the Greek was retained. In due course the biddings vanished and the Kyrie contracted to its present form.
Rev G. E. Glover, Sunderland.

QUESTION: Where can we find the original text and an English translation of the beautiful ANC anthem, 'Nkosi Sikele', and where could we find a full choral recording?

☐ TWO performances given by church congregations are included on the LP, *Let Their Voices Be Heard* (Rounder Records 5024). The accompanying notes refer to the hymn as 'the black national anthem' and include the text, with its verses in three languages – Zulu, Xhosa and Sotho – and a translation.

Text and translation also appear, with the melody line and an indication of chords, in *Culture in Another South Africa*, edited by W. Campschreur and J. Dvendal (Zed Books, London, 1989). Here the hymn is labelled 'the national anthem of South Africa'. In both these sources the translations seem to be partial and somewhat at variance with each other.

Both book and record can be obtained from International Defence and Aid Fund for Southern Africa, 64 Essex Road, London N1.

Peter Best, School of Languages, Polytechnic of Central London, London NW1.

☐ THERE is a lovely version in the soundtrack to the film, *Cry Freedom* (MCA Records: LP MCG 6029; tape MCGC 6029).

Philip Longwell, Wells-next-Sea, Norfolk.

☐ A SINGLE called 'Nkosi Sikele' iAfrica' – God Bless Africa – is being released on Monday 26 February. This song is from the film, *Cry Freedom*, recorded by George Fenton and Jonas Gwanga. Catalogue number MCA 1228.

John V. Roy, MCA Records, London W1.

☐ MUSIC and a translation can be found in *In Township Tonight – South Africa's Black City Music and Theatre*, by David P. Coplan (Longman ISBN 0 582 644003).

Paul Bull, Leicester.

☐ ENOCH Sontonga, a teacher at the Methodist Mission School at Klipspruit, 11 miles from Johannesburg, wrote the hymn in 1897. Shortly after the founding of the ANC in 1912, it was adopted as its anthem.

The same tune is met in many parts of southern Africa and is used for the Zambian national anthem. My wife and I taught at Chipembi and Kafue nearly 30 years ago but an abiding memory is of the haunting refrain of 'Nkosi Sikele' iAfrika', sung by our pupils with instinctive harmonies and untaught talent in a beautiful diminuendo.

David Radcliffe, Southport, Merseyside.

QUESTION: Who was the first man to do what a man's gotta do, when did he do it and what was it when he'd done it?

☐ THE words are often, wrongly, attributed to John Wayne. They were, in fact, uttered by Shane (Alan Ladd) in the film of the same name.

What Shane has to do, in the conscious sense, is kill Wilson (Jack Palance) *et al.*, and pave the way for a peaceful existence for his friends, the homesteaders. However, there is an undercurrent, touched on in the movie but camouflaged by the superb action scenes and atmospheric location. It is more fully developed in the novel, *Shane*, by Jack Schaeffer, which shows that Shane is obviously in love with his friend's wife (Jean Arthur). There is also a hint that she may be falling in love with Shane while retaining her love for her husband, Joe (Van Heflin). Therefore Shane must do two things for his friends: he must rid the range of villains, at the cost of his life perhaps; and he must take himself out of their lives for ever. This is what a man has to do, and do it he does.
R. A. Southern, Wigan, Lancs.

☐ I DON'T think your correspondent is quite right in attributing the phrase to Alan Ladd in *Shane*. He uses *similar* expressions like 'A man has to be what he is' and 'I couldn't do what I gotta do', but never the exact words.

The expression does occur in John Steinbeck's *Grapes of Wrath* in Chapter 18 (p. 206 of the Penguin edition) when Casy says 'I know this – a man got to do what he got to do.' This was published in 1939, which predates *Shane* anyway. Yours pedantically
Stephen Collins, Ripon, Yorks.

QUESTION: Is Syd Barrett (founder member of Pink Floyd) still alive?

☐ ANY rumour of his death was a gross exaggeration. He is alive and well, and living happily in Cambridge. He spends most of his time thinking, writing and painting.

He has no further active interest in music, and wishes to be left to lead a quiet life.
Alan J. Barrett (elder brother of Syd), Cambridge.

QUESTION: Has any evidence been produced to compare the divorce rate among couples joined in holy matrimony and those married in a Register Office?

☐ As a full-time divorce lawyer and, curiously, a part-time registrar of marriages, I have not observed any significant difference in the respective divorce rates during the 15 or so years in which I have been involved in joining happy couples and unjoining unhappy ones.

However, second marriages can fail as well as first ones and there is no doubt that the majority of second marriages take place in a register office, because of the reluctance of most churches to effect the remarriage of a divorcee. For this reason I would suspect that in purely numerical terms, register office marriages produce more divorces.
Donald G. Garrick, Beverley, North Humberside.

QUESTION: What was the origin of the old debate about how many angels can dance on the head of a pin?

☐ This poetical and interesting question was raised by Thomas Aquinas (1225-1274). He is known as the Father of Moral Philosophy and also as the Angelic Doctor because of his preoccupation with the qualities, nature and behaviour of these celestial beings. He was canonised in 1323.
Muriel Cottrell, Wirral, Merseyside.

☐ IT IS often used disparagingly about theological speculation. In a long past BBC 'Brains Trust' session, the late
Prof C. E. M. Joad used the expression in that way. The
following week he was firmly denounced for loose thinking by a listener who claimed, with apparent authority,
that there was no evidence that this subject was ever
debated. On the other hand, he said, monks in medieval
times would, purely as a recreation, hold rigidly struc-
tured debates on all kinds of unlikely subjects. So the
'angels' debate could have originated from such a source.
Joad had, it seemed, no answer to that. Nor have I – it just
stays in the memory from the old 'Brains Trust' days.
Stephen Fearnley, Halifax, W. Yorks.

☐ I WAS interested to read the comments on this dispute.
However, I think the idea behind it was whether angels
had dimensions and occupied space. If they did not, then
clearly an infinity of angels could dance on the sharpest,
most needle-fine point. Milton gets round the difficulty
most beautifully in Book One of *Paradise Lost* when he
makes the Fallen Angels appear first 'In bigness to sur-
pass Earth's Giant Sons' and then to 'throng numberless'
in Pandemonium like tiny elves – 'incorporeal Spirits'.
Laura Garratt, Uxbridge, Middx.

QUESTION: What are the origins of the CND logo?

☐ THE symbol was originally designed by Gerald Holtom for the first Aldermaston march in 1958, organised
by the Direct Action Committee Against Nuclear War. It
incorporates the semaphore for N and D.
Radhika Holmstrom, Press Officer, CND, London N1.

☐ IT IS the old Nazi death sign, representing the World
Ash Tree (The Tree Yggdrasil) from Nordic mythology,
with its three great roots. One ended in Hel, the realm of
the dead. One ended in Riesenheim, the realm of the

giants. One ended in Asgard, the realm of the gods. It is illustrated in David Littlejohn's *Foreign Legions of the Third Reich,* Vol II, page 201.

In later years, CND changed the device on their badge to the 1940 divisional insignia of Hitler's 3rd Panzer division. The man responsible for CND wearing the old Nazi insignia was the late Gerald Holtom (he was also responsible for that extremely durable lie about semaphore). What his motives were we shall probably never know. It is not impossible that it was a rather sinister joke.
Shamus O. D. Wade, London W3.

QUESTION: Was Chekhov really 6ft 4in tall, as I read recently?

☐ No, there was a short Chekhov. He existed as certainly as a plump Pickwick or a square Archbishop of Canterbury. How dreadful would be the world if Chekhov were a lumbering giant towering over his uncle Vanya and frightening his three sisters! Would their cherries be safe from a 6ft 4in monster Chekhov?

Believe in a giant Chekhov! You might as well believe in a midget Rasputin. You may set all the literary scholars in the world to measure Chekhov but what would their results prove? We see the Chekhov we want to see.
Pharcellus Lennon, London N19.

☐ An 1879 official Change of Residence permit gives the height of Chekhov, at age 19, as 'two arshins, nine vershoks' – apparently 5ft 11in. The lad could have growed or it could have been a bureaucratic error. But what's a few vershoks between friends?
W. L. Kendall, South Shields, Tyne and Wear.

QUESTION: What does the K stand for in Jerome K. Jerome? I have seen it given as Klapka, but I am sure I heard on a radio programme that it was Kafka, because Kafka was a friend of the Jerome family.

☐ SINCE Jerome K. Jerome was born 24 years before Franz Kafka, he can hardly have been named after him.
Edwin Chapman, Reading.

☐ JKJ WAS registered, a month after his birth, in his father's names: Jerome Clapp Jerome. Clapp came from 'Clapa, a Dane who lived in the neighbourhood of Bideford, Devonshire, about the year AD 1000' [*Jerome K. Jerome.* Alfred Moss, Selwyn and Blount, 1928]. The family informally added the name Klapka, and this replaced the Clapp.
C. R. T. Nankivell, Kingstanding, Birmingham.

☐ THE Avenell (formerly Penguin) *Companion to English and American Literature* gives the middle name as Klapka, after a Hungarian general who was a friend of the writer's father.
Alun Rees, Cardiff.

QUESTION: Who first lay back and thought of England?

☐ ALICE, Lady Hillingdon, in her journal, 1912: 'I am happy now that Charles calls on my bedchamber less frequently than of old. As it is, I now endure but two calls a week and when I hear his steps outside my door I lie down on my bed, close my eyes, open my legs and think of England.'
N. G. Macbeth, Kenilworth.

QUESTION: Where are they now: the library books that Joe Orton defaced and for which he spent six months in jail?

□ A COLLECTION of the book jackets is in the Islington Local History Collection, Central Reference Library, 2 Fieldway Crescent, London N5 1PF (telephone: 071-609 3051). Orton was prosecuted by Islington Libraries for defacing book jackets and for using book plates to decorate his walls. The original jackets are now very fragile but photographic copies can be seen by anyone who makes an appointment to do so.
Val Dawson, Area Librarian, London N5.

QUESTION: What is the origin of the phrase 'as sick as a parrot'?

□ TO AVOID United States quarantine and livestock importing restrictions, people smuggling parrots from South America into the US dope the birds on tequila as they near the Mexican border. Careful timing of the binge

will ensure that the birds are sleeping it off through the border crossing formalities and will not greet the officials with a mouthful of verbals as is the breed's wont. Having thus avoided detection, the downside for the exotic loud-mouths is coming to with the mother and father of a hangover. This queasiness manifests itself in the origin of the expression.

F. L. O'Toole, London SW19.

□ THE phrase originates from 1926 when the previously obscure disease of bird psittacosis became a pandemic of clinical importance, involving humans in 12 countries with more than 800 cases. The association of respiratory infections in man and contact with parrots was soon recognised.

Dr F. W. A. Johnson, Liverpool.

□ IT IS a corruption of 'sick as a pierrot' and refers to the typically pale and miserable face of that French panto-mime character.

Peter Barnes, Milton Keynes.

☐ ANOTHER theory (but a quite erroneous one) is that the Amazon parrot – a large green bird with yellow cheeks – was the most-sickly looking creature imaginable.
(Mrs) Jane M. Glossop, Pwllheli, Gwynedd.

☐ I FIRST heard this simile shortly after the Monty Python 'Norwegian Blue' sketch. Whether this is relevant, or whether it is just another example of people finding *non-sequitur* expressions of this type amusing, I know not. My mother always used to be as sick as a cowboy's 'oss. The interesting thing is that being sick as a parrot is not the same as being sick as a dog.
Alex Wilson, Billingham, Cleveland.

QUESTION: Why are British elections always held on Thursdays?

☐ UNTIL 1918, polling at General Elections took place over several days and at one time different constituencies could complete polling on different days, thereby – it was alleged – creating a bandwagon effect for a successful political party. The 1918 Representation of the People Act restricted polling to one day (except for Orkney and Shetland until 1929). Since 1918 a General Election has always been on a Thursday, except for 1918, 1922, 1924 and 1931. The reason for choosing Thursday, it is said, was as follows.

On Fridays the voters were paid their wages and if they went for a drink in a public house they would be subject to pressure from the Conservative brewing interests, while on Sundays they would be subject to influence by Free Church ministers who were generally Liberal in persuasion. Therefore choose the day furthest from influence by either publicans or Free Church clergymen, namely Thursday. Although these influences are much less significant today, the trend towards Thursday becoming a universal polling day has continued, because Urban District Councils and Rural District Councils all polled on a Saturday until they were abolished under the 1972 Local Government Act. Their successor District Councils poll on a Thursday and the Parish Council polling day was changed from Saturday to Thursday at the same time.

E. M. Syddique (Research and Information Department), Electoral Reform Society, London SE1.

☐ BRITISH elections aren't held only on Thursdays. General elections have been held on a Thursday only since 1935: before then, any weekday was used – or even a Saturday, as in 1918. By-elections, too, can be held on any day except a Sunday , although there have been only two since 1965 not held on a Thursday; Manchester Exchange in 1973 and Hamilton in 1978 (because the World Cup started on the Thursday), both on a Wednesday.

Using Thursday is a convention, rather than a rule, so the reason for it is open to argument. I've always presumed it had something to do with Friday being pay-day, giving voters an incentive to go out and do their civic duty and get 'rewarded' for it the next day. Of the 74 post-war by-elections not held on a Thursday, only two were held on a Friday, two on a Saturday and three on a Monday, compared to 29 on a Tuesday and 38 on a Wednesday. If pay-packets were conventionally delivered on a Thursday, Wednesday would doubtless be the convention for elections.

L. Raphael, Kilmaurs, Strathclyde.

QUESTION: The words of Beethoven's 'Ode to Joy' in his 9th Symphony begin 'Freude, schöner Götterfunken'. It is said that at first the word was not 'Freude'

(joy) but 'Freiheit' (freedom), later changed for political reasons. Can anyone enlighten me?

□ FRIEDRICH von Schiller, poet, playwright, philosopher, army surgeon and professor of history wrote his 'Ode to Joy' in 1785. It consists of eight stanzas of eight lines, each accompanied by a different chorus of four lines. It wasn't until about 1819 that Beethoven conceived the idea of using three or so verses as a finale to his D minor symphony. The whole poem is concerned with joy, bliss, pleasure as the driving force on earth and heaven.

It was Professor Gerald Abraham in this century who suggested that, on the eve of the French Revolution, Schiller would have been thinking of *Freiheit* rather than *Freude.* However, Lord Lytton (then Sir Edward), publishing his translations of Schiller's poetry in 1844, prefaces the 'Hymn to Joy' with: 'The origin of the Hymn is said to be this: Schiller, when at Leipzig, or its vicinity, saved a poor student of theology, impelled by destitution and the fear of starvation, from drowning himself in the river Pleisse. Schiller gave him what money he had; obtained his promise to relinquish the thought of suicide, at least while the money lasted; and a few days afterwards, amidst the convivialities of a marriage feast, related the circumstances so as to affect all present. A subscription was made, which enabled the student to complete his studies, and ultimately to enter into an official situation. Elated with the success of his humanity, it is to Humanity that Schiller consecrated this Ode.'
R. G. Daniels, Northampton.

QUESTION: What is a rostrum camera and why, judging by the credits on all TV channels, does only Ken Morse have one?

*Face behind the name: Ken Morse with his
rostrum camera*

☐ KEN Morse is almost certainly too busy to explain, so I'll try to do it for him. Ken has a solid bench ('rostrum') with a camera (film or video) firmly mounted above it. Both bench and camera can be moved in relation to one another, sometimes in quite complex ways, and often under computer-control. This arrangement allows precision cinematography of all kinds of things a director might find useful: for example, a slow and elegant move from a wide-shot of a music score to a huge close-up of Beethoven's scribbled 'Muss es sein? Es muss sein.' This sort of thing is often difficult to shoot on location – either because you didn't know the precise timing needed; or because you hadn't even thought of it.

The reason everyone goes to Ken Morse used to be that he had a parrot. Now it's simply because he's good, fast, and doesn't rip you off. He also exercises a certain degree of editorial control. I once hired him to shoot 12 transpar-

encies of Mayan hieroglyphics on loan from the British
Museum, and he filmed only six. When I phoned to ask
about the others, he told me that six was enough for any
TV programme. I used four.
Christopher Sykes, London SW13.

☐ No, Ken Morse does not have the only one.
*Millard Parkinson, Rostrum Camera Dept, Granada TV,
Manchester.*

**QUESTION: Why is nail varnish removed from
fingers and toes, even during minor operations unre-
lated to hands and feet?**

☐ INTENSIVE electronic monitoring of all anaesthetised
patients is essential, but the most important monitor is
the anaesthetist, whose observation, knowledge and skill
are the ultimate safeguard for the patient. Ignoring
important matters such as keeping the patient asleep, the
single essential of anaesthesia is that the circulating blood
should contain sufficient oxygen to maintain life. The
fingernail bed is a good place to see if the blood is pink
with oxygenated haemoglobin, not the darker, purply-
blue colour of haemoglobin without oxygen. The anaesthetist may ask therefore that nail varnish be removed to
give a clear view of the nail bed.

However, the human eye is notoriously bad at assessing
colour, and the oxygen content may already be danger-
ously low before a change in the colour of circulating
blood can be detected. The pulse oximeter is a non-
invasive device which, clipped to a finger, measures the
degree of oxygenation of the blood to an accuracy of plus
or minus 2 per cent. It has been shown that a pulse
oximeter, by warning the anaesthetist of minor episodes
of low oxygenation, can significantly reduce their inci-
dence and prevent major de-oxygenation. Pulse oxi-

meters can 'see' through nail varnish, and although there have been reports of misreading due to nail varnish, this is unusual and unlikely with the latest equipment. Thus, when a modern pulse oximeter is to be used, nail varnish need not be removed.

However, not all operating theatres are so equipped, and if your anaesthetist does ask you to remove your nail varnish, it is because he is determined to make your anaesthetic safe.

(Dr) John R. Davies, FFARCS, Consultant Anaesthetist, Haverbreaks, Lancaster.

QUESTION: As a Dutchman, I am most interested to find out where expressions like Dutch uncle, Dutch courage, etc came from.

☐ THERE is no exact 'origin' *per se*, but during the late seventeenth century England fought a series of naval wars with the Dutch, and these phrases originated about then, based on a popular dislike of the national enemy. What the phrases have in common is a reference to something that is either false or deathly boring. A few which were popular at the time include 'Dutch consolation', meaning no consolation at all, and 'I hear the Dutch have captured Holland', meaning that the news is already known to the hearer and is stale. The questioner may be pleased to know, however, that while the English invented the insults, the Dutch won all the battles.

Morgen Witzel, Leigh, Kent.

☐ BREWSTER'S *Dictionary of Phrase and Fable* lists no fewer than 25 expressions concerning the Dutch, of which five are suggestive of Dutch alcoholism, and a further four imply disdain towards the Netherlands. One of my best friends is a native of the province of Noord Brabant, so speaking from experience I would say that to this day the

people of the Netherlands certainly enjoy a drink, and if that isn't the case then I'm a Dutchman.
Sue Anderson, Basingstoke, Hants.

QUESTION: Does the Rubicon still exist?

☐ THE Rubicon is a small stream rising in the foothills of the Etruscan Apennines to enter the Adriatic Sea at the resort of Gatteo a Mare, some ten miles north of Rimini. It formed the southern boundary of the province of Cisalpine Gaul with the Roman Republic, and so its crossing by Julius Caesar in January 49 BC was effectively a declaration of war on his rival, Pompey, who commanded the armies of the Roman senate. The stream's identity was once a source of some dispute, the Uso, the Piscatello and the Fiumicino di Savignano all being the subjects of rival claims. The Uso was awarded the name by a Papal Bull of 1756, but a comparison of distances with the accounts of Suetonius, Plutarch and Lucan led to the Fiumicino being officially renamed the Rubicon in 1932.
James Elliot, British Library Map Library, London WC1.

☐ NOWADAYS travellers in this part of the world are better catered for than Julius Caesar was in 49 BC when he crossed the Rubicon, as they can stop off for a snack at the Rubicone service station on the A14 autostrada between the Cesna and Rimini interchanges.
Keith Spence, Tunbridge Wells, Kent.

QUESTION: In the film, *Brief Encounter* (original version), which locations were used for the high street, the hospital, the boating lake and the station(s)?

☐ THE location of the film is intended to be that of a

typical Home Counties town, the model for which we believe to be Weybridge in Surrey, where Noël Coward himself grew up. However, some of the film was shot in the north; certainly the station is that of Carnforth in Lancashire. We cannot be sure of the other locations, but it seems possible that these are to be found in Lancashire rather than Surrey. Leslie Halliwell, in the book, *Halliwell's Hundred,* says that the film is 'full of little indications, perhaps unintentioned, that the setting is northern'.

Nigel Parkin and Andrew Willis, Nottingham.

☐ CARNFORTH was the only station in the country which fulfilled the requirements necessary to the plot.
S. Seed, Lancaster.

☐ THE identification of Carnforth station in Lancashire can hardly be an unintentional indication of a northern setting – a train destination board for Hellifield, Skipton, Leeds and Bradford stays in shot easily long enough to be read. Other scenes with a northern flavour include the bridge over a stream and the hospital street of stone houses.

But I thought everyone knew the boating lake was Regent's Park, while the doctor's flat is of a Thirties style common in parts of London. The cinema interior is one of those near Victoria, I believe, and was told at the time that an entrance to Denham Studios was used for the exterior. So for my Home Counties-type settings, such as the fake half- timbered High Street with its Boots, I would look near Denham.
Paul M. S. Hopkins, Epping, Essex.

☐ THE location of some of the High Street shots was Beaconsfield, Bucks. I still remember the odd sensation of leaving the cinema in Beaconsfield New Town, after seeing the film, and walking down the street past shops which I had just seen on the screen. Alas, many of the shops are now estate agents' offices, and Boots, the 'library chemist', is now a Chinese restaurant. However, the pseudo-Tudor beams above what was Batter Fish Shop still remain. Beaconsfield, Gerrards Cross and, of course, Denham Studios, were well known to many film stars who lived in the area, and I wonder if that was the attraction of Beaconsfield.

(Mrs) Mary R. Brook, High Wycombe, Bucks.

QUESTION: Can anyone explain why sex had to enter into some languages? Why, for example, do the French sit on a masculine bench at a feminine table?

☐ THE original Indo-Europeans classified things into male objects, which act on other things or change them; female objects, which bring other things into existence; and childish (that is, neuter) objects, which have no effect on other things but only have things done to them. Thus the earth and the sea are feminine, weapons and tools masculine.

In German, diminutives are neuter. Because neuter objects could not do anything they could never be the subject of the sentence and could not have a nominative case. Even now the nominative is the same as the accusative. The Germans regard the sun as feminine because in northern Europe it is a gentle entity which appears in the spring and coaxes the plants out of the ground. The moon is a masculine object that tells the mighty ocean to come and go. In Italy, on the other hand, the sun is much more like Ra, and will frizzle your brain if you go out without your hat. And in the Mediterranean there are no tides.

I suppose the French bench is masculine because it carries the diners and the table is feminine because it is thought to produce the goodies thereon.

John Ward, Bristol, Avon.

☐ SEX does not really enter into the question of gender in French and similar languages. Most European languages put nouns into either two or three genders, and the real world category that is most nearly related to gender is that of sex. English tends to make females feminine, males masculine, and sexless items neuter. It comes closer to a one-to-one correspondence than other natural languages. However, even English can still treat any powerful or fast-moving machine as feminine, and some animals have obligatory genders, disregarding their sex (Jenny wren and Robin redbreast, Jack daw and Mag pie).

German, as Mark Twain pointed out, has neuter for 'young lady' (das Fräulein), and feminine for 'turnip' (die Rübe). Latin, the parent of French, had three genders with the same sort of 'fits where it touches' match as has German today. As French evolved from Latin, the endings of words were 'eroded', and neuter singulars ceased to be distinguished from masculine singulars, neuter plurals from feminine singulars, leaving only two genders, so that – regardless of sex – all nouns must be either masculine or feminine. 'Table' comes from 'tabula', which was already feminine in Latin. 'Banc' (bench) is derived from the same Germanic word that gives us bench, which was (and is) feminine, but like many foreign borrowings was taken as masculine.

W. S. Dodd, Language Centre, University of Exeter.

☐ ONE theory is that man's fantasy personalised and personified everything, and hence bestowed on every object, even inanimate ones, the qualities of a man or woman. The great and powerful was seen as possessed by male attributes, and smaller and weaker seen as possessed by female ones. Eventually this notion survived in modern language.

A second theory is that it was the sex of the pronoun which accompanied the noun, i.e. his or hers, which became transferred to that noun.

A third theory has also been advanced, based on the recorded fact that among some primitive people (for instance, Latin American tribes) two languages existed side by side, a male and female one. Thus an object would be called by a different word depending on whether a man or woman spoke of it. With the passage of time the two languages became merged but the idea of gender survived. A question that arises is why did men and women have separate languages in the first place? It is quite likely that the tribes' females came from another part of the country or another tribe altogether. Their presence might have been due to them having been captured as the spoils of war. The language that they spoke would have been foreign to the men and impregnated with their sex. Similar events would evolve due to the practice of marrying women from another tribe.
Alan Willmott, Cheltenham, Glos.

QUESTION: Who was Riley and why does living his life sound so desirable, in spite of dissolute overtones?

☐ THE saying comes from a comic song, 'Is That Mr Reilly?' (sic), which was popular in the US in the 1880s. There was also a music-hall song in England at about the same time: 'Are You The O'Reilly?' One was probably a variant of the other. The latter includes the lines 'Are you the O'Reilly they speak of so highly? Cor blimey, O'Reilly, you are looking well.'
Stephen Pratt, Twyford, Berks.

QUESTION: I know the reason for having the extra day every four years. But why February 29?

□ THE Julian Calendar, introduced by Julius Caesar, was a straightforward affair. The first month of the year, March, had 31 days and subsequent months had 30 or 31 days alternately, except for the last month, February, for which only 29 days remained, increased to 30 on leap year.

This lasted until Augustus came along and decided to follow Julius's example and name a month after himself. He then noticed that the month he had chosen only had 30 days, whereas July, after Julius, had 31.

This was not acceptable to Augustus, so August was increased to 31 days and poor old February only had 28 days left or 29 in a leap year.

G. D. Morris, Sutton Coldfield, W. Midlands.

QUESTION: Whatever happened to the *Oz* trio, Richard Neville, Felix Dennis and Jim Anderson?

□ RICHARD Neville has returned to Australia and, in 1988, was working in television and living with his wife and daughter in a house called 'Happy Daze' (good name, eh?).

Felix Dennis has become the most materially successful of the *Oz* defendants, using his underground press expertise to form an international publishing company, specialising in martial arts, TV and film tie-ins, and computers. Homes in London, New York and Europe go with his manor house and Rolls-Royce.

Jim Anderson emigrated to the USA in 1974 and lives in Bolinas. For all the above information read the excellent book on the 1960s London underground scene, *Days In The Life*, by Jonathon Green.

Arthur Clifford, Southall, Middx.

□ JIM Anderson has written a rich and enthralling novel about a young boy in Australia in wartime. It was pub-

lished by Grafton Books in 1989 as *Billarooby*, and is available in the UK for £12.95.
A. Copping, London.

QUESTION: Why do the British drive on the left and other countries on the right?

☐ THE left is the natural side to ride if you are on horseback. Mounting a horse is done from the left, so that a sword (worn on the left by right-handed men) will not get in the way. If you mount from a mounting block or the verge on the left, it is natural to set off on the left-hand side of the road.
Christine Moore, London SW4.

☐ THERE is a theory that the change to the right came about with fire-arms, which are fired from the right shoulder, thus aimed to the left. Certainly a major proponent of keeping to the right was Napoleon Bonaparte, who whether for military reasons or personal custom, imposed keeping to the right wherever he went. In the twentieth century it was another dictator that imposed keeping to the right wherever he went: Adolf Hitler. In his birthplace in Austria and in Czechoslovakia signs reading 'Rechts fahren' (drive right) were put up when the Nazis moved in. So by keeping to the left we are sticking to our British independence.
Noel Ellis, London SE15.

☐ IMPLICIT in the question is the suggestion that Britain is alone in this particular practice. In fact, over 40 countries drive on the left.
Nicholas Pritchard, Southampton.

QUESTION: I have heard of people exchanging homes for a holiday through an agency, but they have

always been exchanges between here and abroad. Is it possible to exchange within this country?

☐ YES, all that is necessary is a copy of the directory published annually by the various organisations concerned, such as Homelink International of Huntingdon, Cambs. Obviously there are more entries from those wishing to exchange overseas, but anyone can put in an entry giving their preference for Britain, and many people do.
(Mrs) M. Cullingham, Windsor, Berks.

☐ WRITE to the secretary of your political party in the town nearest to where you want to go, state what you can offer and the type of accommodation you need, and ask if anyone is interested in exchanging. We did this last year, had an offer by return of post, and spent a marvellous 10 days in Scotland.
J. and G. Muirhead, Devizes.

☐ THE National Women's Register runs a house exchange scheme for holidays. The current organiser is Jackie Sayers, 18 Broadwater Avenue, Letchworth, Herts SG6 3HE.

If you want to join you will have to become an NWR member (£4 per annum). Details of local organisers can be obtained by ringing the national office, 021-711 3746.
Janet Tuffs, Grantham, Lincs.

QUESTION: We used to hear of a 'clock' whose imaginary hands were moved ever closer to midnight as the arms race continued, midnight denoting the final catastrophe. Is it still going, and what is the time now?

☐ THE Doomsday Clock is operated by the Bulletin of Atomic Scientists in the US and is used to reflect tensions between the superpowers. The clock, which is made of bronze, has a map of the world for a face. The hour hand is positioned permanently at midnight while the minute hand describes the planet's nuclear destiny in minutes from 15 to zero. In the light of recent reforms in Eastern Europe, the board of the Bulletin has agreed to put the minute hand back four minutes to 10 minutes to 12. Very timely!

K. T. McVeigh, Belfast.

QUESTION: Does anyone know of a charity that distributes A-level and degree textbooks to the Third World?

☐ THE Ranfurly Library Service sends books of all levels and types to less developed countries. Founded in 1954, it sends about 600,000 books overseas every year. The books are donated by individuals, schools, libraries, publishers, etc, in the UK. They are carefully sorted, irrelevant material is pulped and the rest is sent out in response to detailed specifications from the requesting bodies.

David Membrey, Deputy Director, Ranfurly Library Service, 2 Coldharbour Place, 39/41 Coldharbour Lane, London SE5 9NR. Tel: 071-733 3577.

☐ RANFURLY Library Service has an agreement with the national Rotary association for local Rotary clubs to collect and transport books to London.

A. Zalewska, Department of Educational Support Services, Huddersfield Technical College.

QUESTION: Does anybody know anything about the unfortunate man in this engraving (overleaf) – 'Samuel Wood (The Miller)' – and his injury?

☐ SAMUEL Wood from Worcestershire was employed by a miller on the Isle of Dogs. In August 1737, he was caught in the machinery and his arm was torn off. The

Samuel Wood: a miller's tale

original version of the print was sold at this time to raise funds for him.

The design is allegorical, and is intended to show that Wood had a narrow escape and was 'half-dead' – i.e. half of his body is hidden, because he stands in his own open grave, shown in front of him, but he turns his head away from it to indicate he rejects death at this time. The vignette shows him in early Georgian costume trapped in the cogs of the mill wheel. In 1820 the engraving was re-issued, together with a short account of Wood, in Vol 4 of Caulfield's *Remarkable Characters*.

After his accident – which he survived more than 25 years – Wood became a publican and Customs House officer in London.
Richard Adaway, Manchester.

☐ WOOD had his arm torn from his body as a result of a rope winding round it. The other end was fastened to the cogs of a mill. The arteries and nerves were drawn out of the body and the vessels, having been stretched, bled very little. The first surgeon to treat the patient placed the vessels within the wound and applied a simple dressing.

Samuel Wood was then admitted to St Thomas' Hospital in London. The dressings were not removed for a number of days and the patient had no severe symptoms. On examination it was found that the remaining skin had been enough to cover the wound and that it had healed of its own accord.

This case was described by William Cheselden, surgeon at St Thomas' Hospital, in his book, *The Anatomy of the Human Body*, published in 1756. The preparation of flaps of skin and tissue to cover the wound following the amputation was a method preferred by Cheselden. The case provided him with a useful example to help verify his theories.
Michael Tambini, The Operating Theatre Museum, London SE1.

☐ AN account may be found in the *Philosophical Transactions of the Royal Society*, Vol 40, p. 313, by John Belcher, FRS. Presumably the detail in the engraving is accurate, since Wood's arm was preserved in spirits after the accident.
K. Moore, Archivist, The Royal Society, London SW1.

QUESTION: A catalytic converter in my car will convert poisonous carbon monoxide into carbon dioxide. Since carbon dioxide is thought to be the

major cause of the greenhouse effect, am I really being 'green' if I use one?

□ IT IS 'green' to use a catalytic converter, but it is only the second of three important steps. The first is to use unleaded fuel. The second is to use the 'cat' which removes from the exhaust gases much of not only carbon monoxide but of other pollutants as well. This does increase emissions of carbon dioxide, and there is only one solution to this, i.e. to burn less fuel. Thus the third step is to ensure that your car is as economical with fuel as possible (no high-performance gas-guzzlers); use public transport whenever and wherever you can; combine your car usage with other people whenever you can; use a light foot on the accelerator and keep both acceleration and speed down. One day we might have really pollution-free vehicles, but until we do we must make the best of what we have.
L. H. Watkins, Crowthorne, Berks.

□ THE questioner is right that catalytic converters do nothing to prevent emissions of carbon dioxide. They may help to reduce global warming in a small way, as catalytic converters remove carbon monoxide and oxides of nitrogen whose emissions would otherwise lead to a build-up of tropospheric ozone; unlike stratospheric ozone (some 20 km above our heads) tropospheric ozone is both a toxin and an effective greenhouse gas. However, carbon dioxide accounts for about half of the enhanced greenhouse effects and, in the UK, road transport accounts for about one quarter of our emissions of CO_2. The only way of preventing your car emitting CO_2 is to stop using it.
Dr Keith Shine, Department of Meteorology, Reading University.

□ CATALYTIC converters kid people into believing their

cars are eco-friendly. This is a false premise. For a start, catalytic converters do not start to function until the engine reaches a working temperature of 300°C and will not perform optimally until 1000°C. As the majority of car journeys are of five miles or less (Source: Dept of Transport's *National Travel Survey 1985-6*) engines rarely get much past the first temperature. Using a car − no matter how catalytically-converted − can never be Green. Get a bike instead.

Carlton Reid, Editor, Whole Life, Newcastle Upon Tyne.

☐ THE burning of petrol in car engines always produces carbon dioxide (CO_2), along with a small amount (1-4 per cent) of carbon monoxide (CO). The CO which escapes from your car exhaust will eventually oxidise to CO_2 in the atmosphere anyway; a catalyst simply speeds up the process in order to reduce the local health effects of CO.

So overall there should be no net effect on CO_2 emissions except that the use of catalysts is incompatible with certain engine types, such as the 'lean-burn' design, which offer greater fuel efficiency (and thus lower CO_2 emissions) but are unable to meet emission limits for other pollutants. The only effective way to alleviate greenhouse guilt syndrome is to use less petrol. Buy a more fuel-efficient car or, better still, a bicycle.

Tim Brown, National Society for Clean Air, Brighton.

QUESTION: Who was the first April Fool?

☐ THE tradition of the trickster in northern Europe goes right back to our pre-Christian religion. In the Norse mythology, the prankster-god Loki can be disruptive towards the other gods but able to carry out tasks no other can. He represents the need to question and challenge authority so that patterns of thought and behaviour

do not become stale or accepted uncritically. Loki is traditionally thought of as patron god of April.
Andy Lawton, Chesterfield, Derbys.

□ WHEN Vasco da Gama arrived in Calicut in March 1498 (not in May as is commonly thought), he could not have known that he was creating the first documented April Fool. He was invited to the Feast of Huli, on the last day of March. The chief amusement was the be-fooling of people by sending them on fruitless and foolish errands. As any fool knows, Vasco da Gama was sent by the Hindu Rajah of Malabar inland looking for cloves and pepper in any area where they did not grow, but the event is not always attributed to the date of his return – the morning of April 1.
A. J. G. Glossop, Pwllheli, Gwynedd.

QUESTION: Which anthology includes what must surely be the most beautiful love poem in the world, 'Black Marigolds', translated from the Sanskrit by E. Powys Mather?

□ THE poem, by Bilhana, is on pages 47-58 of *An Anthology of World Poetry*, edited by Van Doren, Cassell, 1929 (3rd edition 1941). Over 1,200 pages for 8s 6d. I agree about the poem.
E. H. Seagroatt, Liverpool 14.

□ GRANGER'S *Index to Poetry* gives two anthologies of which the more recent is *Erotic Poetry* edited by William Cole (Random House 1963). This query, as with many others appearing in 'Notes and Queries', can be answered quickly by the public library service. But, of course, I am biased.
Mike Gibson, Assistant County Librarian, Scarborough, N. Yorks.

QUESTION: What is Semtex? Is the power of this explosive really as great as journalists would have us believe?

☐ SEMTEX is the Czechoslovakian trade name for an explosive known as pantaerithrytol tetranitrate, C (CH$_2$ ONO$_2$) or PETN. It is manufactured by different companies around the world under licence, and is one of the most powerful explosives of its kind.
Eric Alex Roberts, Ashton-under-Lyne, Lancs.

☐ SEMTEX is a plastic explosive manufactured by the Semtin munitions works in central Czechoslovakia. Its high media profile results from its prized characteristics of malleability (it is putty-like), safety in handling and, most notably, its lack of smell, making it undetectable by sniffer dogs. As such, it is a perfect terrorist weapon, and is regularly claimed to have been found in IRA arms caches, with the suggestion that it is sourced from the Czechs via Libya.

Or is it? Is all 'Semtex' Semtex? The bizarre claim is made that Semtex is unique. The idea that a second-division industrial power (even a major arms exporter like Czechoslovakia) can produce a substance that defies analysis and duplication by Western chemical companies, seems ludicrous.

On the other hand, it would be politically convenient to blame one bogey nation for supplying weapons to a terrorist network, rather than admit the alternative: that Western nations can and do make undetectable explosives, that these are in use in state covert operations (where and against whom?), and that they are regularly stolen from inadequately guarded military bases or police stations by terrorists. Is anyone prepared to confirm this?
Tony Clarke, Ely, Cambs.

QUESTION: Who was Kilroy when he was here, and where is he now?

☐ THE original Kilroy was an inspector at one of the inland shipyards in America where they built 'Liberty Ships'.

Inspection is a responsible job, with lives depending on it. Each weld of the hull has to be inspected as it is completed, because quite often the next step will build some structure internal to the ship that will mask the weld and leave it inaccessible to later inspection.

It was Kilroy's peculiar custom to record his approval of each weld by writing on the weld itself. Along decks and gangways subsequent traffic soon removed his marks, but where internal structures hid them they remained. The result was that among every crew who eventually sailed one of his ships, his became a name to conjure with, an invisible presence among them. Nobody ever met Kilroy face to face, yet he must surely have been there, hiding himself away, because whenever you looked into an unused locker or enclosed space, no matter how small or inaccessible (provided only that it backed on to the hull), he had been and gone just before you, leaving his message freshly chalked on the wall 'Kilroy was here'.
Daniel Lowy, Sutton, Surrey.

☐ 'KILROY was here' is graffiti from the Second World War. James Kilroy was the senior shipyard inspector at the US forces shipping depot at Quincy, Massachusetts, being required to sign for all equipment consigned to ETO (European Theater Operations).

GIs, finding his name on nearly everything they used, started scrawling the phrase wherever they were based. It then spread around the world with the movement of US forces.
Bernard Goodman, London SE1.

☐ ACCORDING to an article by an American journalist,

Susan Ulbing, he was an infantry soldier who got tired of hearing the air force brag that it was always first on the spot. Kilroy specialised in being the first and only one to show up in outrageous places, like the bathroom reserved for Truman, Stalin and Attlee at the Potsdam Conference.
John Idorn, London W8.

QUESTION: What is honey, can it be synthetically produced, and if not, why not?

☐ AFTER visiting a flower, the foraging honey-bee flies back to the hive with the collected fluid in her honey sac, a modified part of the gut. On arrival she regurgitates the fluid and passes it through her mouth to one or more 'house' bees which in turn swallow it and regurgitate it to other house bees, and so on through a chain of bees until the liquid is finally placed in a cell of honeycomb.

As each bee sucks the liquid up a few proteins are added, and water is evaporated. After the liquid is placed in the cell of honeycomb, bees continue to process it, and water evaporates as they do so. The temperature of the hive is around 35°C, and this temperature, and the fanning of bees, causes further water evaporation. When the water content is 20 per cent or less, the honey is considered 'ripe', i.e. it will not ferment, and bees place a wax capping on the cell.
Nicola Broadbear, Troy, Monmouth.

☐ HONEY varies in flavour, colour and viscosity according to the forage crop, and it is our native flora which gives English honey its distinctive flavour. Its composition consists of 18 per cent water, 35 per cent glucose, 40 per cent fructose and 4 per cent other sugars, the remaining 3 per cent being made up of about 15 organic acids including acetic, butyric, gluconic, malic and succinic; about 12 elements including potassium, calcium, sulphur, chlorine and iron; around 17 amino acids including proline, glutanic acid and lysine; and between four and seven proteins.

This information is gleaned from the *Guide to Bees and Honey* by Ted Hooper.
D. R. Johnson, Saffron Walden, Essex.

☐ CAN honey be synthetically produced? Yes and no. A substitute can be produced using cheap corn syrup. However, it could not be compared to real honey carefully produced by your local beekeeper. It would lack the numerous subtle ingredients which give honey its natural goodness and great variety of taste. Try 'real' honey and taste the difference!
Tom Howard, Boothstown, Manchester.

QUESTION: The leader of the British military mission to Russia in 1939 was Admiral Sir Reginald Plunkett-Ernle-Erle-Drax. Is this the longest hyphenated surname in the UK, and how does a man aspire to have such a surname?

☐ THE name of the explorer, Sir Ranulph Twisleton-Wykeham-Fiennes, contains more letters (33) than that queried (32), but with only three barrels to Sir Reginald's four. As to how the name was acquired, many complex names (not necessarily hyphenated) are the result of marriages, alliances and so forth. The Fiennes family was given the name Wykeham in the Civil War, as a reward for preventing the desecration by the Roundheads of William of Wykeham's tomb in Winchester Cathedral.
Arabella McIntyre Brown, Liverpool 17.

☐ OUR formal family name just beats Plunkett-Ernle-Erle-Drax (21 letters) viz: Hovell-Thurlow-Cumming-Bruce (25 letters). Needless to say, we all abbreviate it. When I was up at Trinity College, Cambridge, it was a curiosity much appreciated by tourists passing the hall doors at the foot of the staircase to my rooms to see the whole rigmarole, prefaced 'Hon A. P.' painted upon the lintel, and followed by 'The Earl Kitchener' and 'The Earl Jellicoe'. There's class!

This dotty accumulation derived from the 18th/19th century usage of a husband's hyphenating his wife's name if she was heiress to landed property. In our case H-T also then elected to marry C-B.

Alec Cumming Bruce, Durham.

□ IN the event that you do not receive a suitable explanation from a member of the Drax family, perhaps the chauffeur's daughter can outline the cause of all the hyphens. The Admiral's ancestors were far better at breeding daughters than sons, so that when Miss Plunkett (a relative of Lord Dunsany – the eminent author) married Mr Ernle their daughter was Miss Plunkett-Ernle. She married Mr Erle; their daughter, Miss Plunkett-Ernle-Erle, married Mr Drax and Reginald got all the surnames.

After four or five daughters Reginald begot a son, who is known as plain Mr Drax. He has dismally failed to maintain the family tradition and has four or five sons. His eldest son is married to the Princess Royal's former Lady-in-Waiting, Zara (yes, that's where the name came from) Something-Something. If she threw in her maiden name, her children would be Something-Something-Plunkett-Ernle-Erle-Drax.

Of more value than the admiral's abortive mission to Stalin was his pioneering interest in solar heating (for his swimming pool).

(Ms) V. E. Troy, Chatham, Kent.

□ MY own name comfortably exceeds that of the gallant admiral.

(Brigadier) Dermot Hugh Blundell-Hollinshead-Blundell, BFPO 26.

☐ THE longest multi-barrelled surname on record in England is: Major Leone Sextus Denys Oswolf Fraudati-filius Tollemache-Tollemache-de-Orellana-Plantagenet-Tollemache-Tollemache (1884-1917). If you insist on non-repetitious ones, try this for size: Lady Caroline Jemima   Temple-Nugent-Chandos-Brydges-Grenville (1858-1946).
Steve Arloff, Watford, Herts.

QUESTION: What became of Bjorn Andreson, the beautiful Tadzio in Visconti's *Death in Venice*?

☐ HE IS still working in Stockholm on films, but mainly in television. His death from a drug overdose was reported in *Films in Review* in 1984 – erroneous, of course. Bjorn was just 16 in 1971 when he appeared in *Death in Venice.*

Tadzio made him famous, but he failed to get any other important film roles and concentrated on TV commercials for Sweden and Japan, where *Death in Venice* was a great hit.

His films as a teenager and later as an adult include *Bluff Stop, The Simple-Minded Murderer, Grass Widowers* and *Peas and Whiskers* (all Swedish). His Swedish TV appearances include the series, 'Swedish Crime', and the thriller, 'Splendid Landing'.

Married since 1983, he separated from his wife in 1986, but since 1988 they have been living together again in Stockholm, with their daughter, Robin. Bjorn's famous blond hair is now brown, but he has retained his stunning looks.
Peter Noble, Editor, Screen International, *London NW8.*

QUESTION: Beef sausages, pork sausages, pork and beef sausages. Why not lamb sausages?

☐ LAMB sausages aren't made for a couple of reasons:

(1) The cost of boneless lamb would make lamb sausages somewhere in the region of £2.50 per lb.

(2) The texture of lamb fat means that the sausage inside the skin is rather chewy and the only way to ameliorate this is to add pork, but this tends to overshadow the taste of the lamb.

Some butchers used to make lamb and tomato sausages to use up all their breasts and trims from the neck end, but not many do this now as the old-style butcher's shops decrease in number.

Colin Ward (former butcher), Leatherhead, Surrey.

☐ COME to Sedbergh and you will find lamb and mint sausages. Go to Barnard Castle and in one of the butchers there you can get many varieties, including lamb. Some of the sausages have pork and apple and beef with curry. There is no end to variations to be had in these northern food-loving areas.

Elizabeth Greenfield, Sedbergh, Cumbria.

☐ YOU can find an excellent 'merguez' in a number of butcher shops in London. If this traditional North African sausage is made following the usual recipe it certainly contains mutton, although perhaps not lamb.

R. Merrifield, Geneva.

☐ LAMB sausages have been produced over hundreds of years – mainly in Greece and Turkey – but also in other countries where sausages are air dried and where, for religious or weather reasons, pork is not eaten. In this country, however, because the predominant sausage is fresh, lamb sausages have not caught on in the way they deserve.

When I opened the world's first specialist artificial additive-free fresh sausage shop in Greenwich two years ago I developed two lamb sausage recipes – lamb and rosemary and lamb and mint. From the first day they were a hit and continue to be two of our biggest sellers.

Local butchers shy away from making lamb sausages because of the lack of natural gelatine in the meat. The binding quality of the meat is diminished and the texture of the finished product can be somewhat crumbly. There are natural ways of solving that problem without resorting to chemical additives. The use of free-range eggs is one of them.
Bill O'Hagan, London SE10.

QUESTION: Who said: 'If you are not part of the solution, you must be part of the problem'?

☐ THIS IS a misquotation of Eldridge Cleaver. The correct (full) quote is: 'There is no more neutrality in the world. You either have to be part of the solution, or you're going to be part of the problem.'
T. Siedner, London NW2.

QUESTION: When was the traffic roundabout invented, and by whom?

☐ RAYMOND Unwin in *Town Planning in Practice* (T Fisher Unwin, 1909) shows a 'carrefour à gyration' attributed to Monsieur Eugene Henard in his *Etudes sur les Transformations de Paris.*

This shows a roundabout (right-hand traffic flow) with horse-drawn vehicles circulating around a 'plateau central'. The drawing is dated 1906 and in the accompanying text M Henard is quoted as suggesting that 'subways should be provided for all the footpaths leading to a space in the centre where the passengers could sort themselves and depart along the subway to whichever streets they wished to reach'.

M Henard put foward his ideas as a means of ensuring 'mouvement continu des voitures', and both he and Unwin were writing at a time when the layout of town streets and studies of traffic conflict were exercising brains in several continental countries and the US.
W. W. Mayor, Exeter.

QUESTION: In the film *Royal Wedding* (1953), Fred Astaire is seen in a hotel room dancing first on the floor, then on the walls and ceiling, all in one shot. How was this achieved?

☐ BY mounting the 'room' within a drum, fixing the furniture and camera and then revolving the drum. This gave the impression of the room remaining stationary while Fred Astaire defied gravity.

The proper name for such a shot is a roll. Stanley Kubrick used a very similar idea in *2001: A Space Odyssey* when a space station worker walked full circle, supposedly using Velcro slippers on a special path. See James Monaco's book, *How to Read a Film* (OUP).
Jeremy Robertson, Trowbridge, Wilts.

QUESTION: Why do two Scottish islands – Harris and Lewis – have Welsh names?

☐ THE names are not Welsh. According to Mackenzie's *Scottish Place-Names*, Harris (Gaelic 'na Hearradh') is from the Norse 'heradh', a district with natural boundaries such as hills; Lewis (Gaelic 'Leodhas') means marshland, and comes from Gaelic through Norse.
J. Moreland Craig, Burton-in-Kendal, Cumbria.

Defying gravity: Fred Astaire in Royal Wedding

QUESTION: In our school we have fluorescent lights. If we turn them off at playtime (15 minutes) will we save money?

☐ PUPILS at Wisewood Comprehensive School in Sheffield set out to answer this very question in the science laboratories. Over a two-week period we metered the energy used by a fluorescent light left on continuously and compared it with one switched on or off every 15 minutes over a four-week period (i.e. 'on' for two weeks).

The tube that was switched on and off used only marginally more energy as measured by standard domestic meters. Our conclusion, taking into account extra wear on starters, was that for a short break (morning and afternoon playtime) it was probably better to leave lights on, while at lunchtime it was economic to switch them off. *Kevin Thompson, Rotherham.*

☐ FLOURESCENT tubes are generally much more economic than tungsten filament bulbs. But there is a widespread theory that it does not pay to switch them off for short periods. In all normal circumstances this is not so, and you will save energy and money by switching a tube off whenever it is not needed. There is a solid base to this theory: switching on does cause some slight extra deterioration in the tubes, also the tubes do consume extra electricity when first switched on.

But tubes last for over 5,000 hours of continuous running, or being turned on about 20,000 times. So unless the tube is used for less than 15 minutes at a time on average, you never get to turn it on for 20,000 times before the 5,000 hours have passed and the tube has failed anyway. Also, the initial extra power demand does not last long; consumption is well on the way back down to normal within a minute. The value of the energy saved by turning off will normally more than compensate for the extra electricity used when you turn on again, plus any potential shortening of the life of the tube.

Taking all factors into account, as long as the tube is at all likely to be off for more than a minute, switch off and save energy and money. Otherwise it will only be worth leaving a tube on all the time if it will otherwise be turned both on and off more than about 10 times per hour and have an average 'off' period of less than about three minutes.

(Dr) P. T. Clarke, Energy Efficiency Office, Dept of Energy, London SW1.

QUESTION: Why is water wet?

☐ WATER isn't wet. Wetness is a description of our experience of water; what happens to us when we come into contact with water in such a way that it impinges on our state of being. We, or our possessions, 'get wet'. A less impinging sense experience of water is that it is cold or warm, while visual experience tells us that it is green or blue or muddy or fast-flowing. We learn by experience that a sensation of wetness is associated with water: 'there must be a leak/I must have sat in something.'
Jacqueline Castles, London W2.

☐ ANY fluid could be said to be wet if wetness is a result of the sensation caused by the movement of a fluid over the skin. Have you ever noticed that you can't feel wetness if you hold your hand perfectly still while it is submerged, or that a drop of water on the skin doesn't feel wet?
Chris and Shevvy Ould, Chesterfield, Derbys.

☐ THE wetness of water is thought to be due to its high moisture content.
(Dr) Jason A. Rush, Dept of Mathematics, Edinburgh University.

☐ WATER is wet to make it a more marketable commodity.
Sam McBride-Dick, Colchester.

☐ THE questioner will be little enlightened by the previous replies and you must surely give him or her another chance. Two answers were humorous; two were just wet.

As an amateur photographer, I am familiar with what is, I think properly, called wetting agent, which is added to water – to the final washing after developing and fixing – to make it wet with respect to the surfaces of photographic film. Without this agent the water resides on film in blobs, resulting in drying marks; with it, most of the water drains off and the rest dries evenly.

So in response to the query I would say (a) water isn't always wet; wetness is always relative to a given substance and/or type of surface and (b) as to why it is wet when it is, presumably the answer is in terms of surface tension.

Laurie Hollings, Brighton.

☐ WATER is wet, in the sense of being a liquid which flows easily, because its viscosity is low, which is because its molecules are rather loosely joined together. The sensation of wetness is largely due to the cooling caused by evaporation, and water has a rather high latent heat of vaporisation, which is the amount of heat it removes from its surroundings in order to convert liquid water into water vapour.

John Geake, Handforth, Cheshire.

☐ NONE of the answers given to this question so far quite gets to the chemical explanation for water's 'wetness'. Wetness is here synonymous with 'clingingness' – water wets because it clings.

Water, of course, is molecularly H_2O and this compound of hydrogen and oxygen is electrically neutral. However, there are also in water many free charged hydroxyls (-OH-, negatively charged) and hydrogen ions (H+ positively charged). These charged particles retain the ability to attract other charged particles (with the opposite charge) just as magnets do. In this way they stick or cling, involving other neutral H_2O molecules at the same time. If water was made up entirely of neutral particles it would not cling, or wet, because the compo-

nent elements would 'prefer' to stick to each other rather than to make bonds with other substances.
Ian Flintoff, London SW6.

☐ IAN Flintoff has surely misrepresented the chemistry behind water's properties. Hydroxyl ions and hydrogen ions in water, far from being 'many' are very few (pure water contains some 556 million water molecules for every hydrogen ion). Water molecules are indeed 'electrically neutral' but are highly polar molecules, that is they have a positive 'end' and a negative 'end', though neither 'end' carries a full unit of charge. It is this polarity which causes water molecules to 'stick to' one another and, given the chance, to other molecules of a polar nature.

Other liquids can be wet, even those which contain molecules which are entirely non-polar (e.g. octane, benzine and even liquid nitrogen – don't try 'em!), but only in relation to another substance because wetness is to do with surface tension and that implies an interface between two substances.

For this reason water is rather poor at wetting things: try washing your hands without soap! The molecules of water do prefer to stick to one another than to molecules of other substances but this effect is easily overcome by introducing another substance which interferes with the interactions between the water molecules. This allows the water molecules to interact with the molecules in the other surface instead.
C. A. Mitchell, Reading, Berks.

QUESTION: When was wire invented and when did its use for fencing become general? I remember reading that the invention of barbed wire changed the face of the American West.

☐ ORDINARY wire was invented about 2,000 years ago.

THE INVENTION OF BARBED WIRE GIVES RISE TO THE FASHION FOR RIPPED JEANS.

In 1873 Joseph Glidden, an American farmer, invented barbed wire similar to that in use today. But some other Americans produced primitive forms earlier; the first was probably L. B. Smith of Ohio in 1867. Before the invention and general use of barbed wire, American farmers had to invest as much money in fencing as in livestock. Cowboys saw it as a threat to their occupation. Opposition to its use led to fence-cutting wars in Texas, Wyoming and New Mexico, but the use of barbed wire spread across the plains of America and the stock-farmer replaced the rancher.

Humphrey Phelps, Westbury-on-Severn, Gloucs.

□ BARBED wire was welcomed by the ranchers of the American West for a number of reasons: wire fences were less likely to be trampled by the herds than were wooden

ones (impractical anyway on the treeless range); open-range farming, the only alternative, required the presence of an army of cowhands; herds enclosed by the new fences could be watered from a single well and grazed more effectively; breeding animals could be more carefully controlled, thus upgrading the standards of the stock; and, finally, the ranchers could establish a powerful claim to huge tracts of land for which they had previously had to compete with smaller-scale farmers, growing urban areas and federal government. The tensions thus created led in several instances to violence and loss of life, till President Grover Cleveland was obliged to send in the army to remove unlawful fences.
Steve Duffy, Betws-yn-Rhos, Clwyd.

□ FIERCE controversy surrounded the invention of wire, which, according to Thomas Malham, was invented by him in 1830 at his foundry in Sheffield.

Similar claims were made by a number of other foundry proprietors around that time, although claims by the Frenchman, Jean François Martin, generated the most heated debate, culminating in legal action contesting his right to patent. The matter was never resolved, since Thomas Malham died of 'an inflamed liver' in 1832. His memorial, in Abney Park Cemetery, North London, although now rusted away, was constructed entirely of wire and took the shape of an anvil topped by a falcon.

This information, and more, is available in *Wire, Its History and Application,* by Dr A. Stone.
C. Grafton, London N16.

□ THE answer above is manifest nonsense. Soft metals (copper, silver, gold) were processed into wire at least as early as Pharaonic Egypt. I must presume you mean drawn iron wire. But this was achieved about 1450 in Augsburg.
John Brunner, S. Petherton, Somerset.

QUESTION: When, and especially why, did Cape Kennedy and its space centre revert to the name Cape Canaveral?

☐ PRESIDENT Kennedy visited Cape Canaveral on 16 November 1963 – a week before his assassination. Following his death, President Johnson changed the name of the cape and the Nasa launch pads to Cape Kennedy and the John F. Kennedy Space Center respectively (Executive Order 11129).

Congress tried – unsuccessfully – to reverse this after pressure from the residents, who felt that changing the old Spanish name was wrong.

Finally, on 29 May, 1973, Governor Askew of Florida bowed to public pressure and signed a bill which brought back Canaveral. This was confirmed by the US Board of Geographic Names the following October. The Nasa shuttle facilities on Merritt Island, due north of the cape, remain as the John F. Kennedy Space Center.
Martin Williams, St Albans, Herts.

QUESTION: Can anyone explain the words of the song, 'Green Grow the Rushes-O'? Several of the references are obviously biblical, but who were the lilywhite boys, the rivals, the proud walkers, and the April rainers? What were the symbols at your door, the bright shiners, and the seven stars in the sky?

☐ THE Dilly Song, as it was once known, is one of the most mysterious oral folk songs. Versions were found in German, Flemish, Scots, Breton, Medieval Latin, Hebrew, Moravian, Greek and French traditions. The song is clearly religious, but not originally Christian. The more traditional versions have only 10 verses; the other two have been added to bring it in line with the 12 apostles.

Any definitive list explaining each verse would be misleading. In his book, *Where is Saint George? ... Pagan Imagery in English Folksong*, Bob Stewart devotes some 6,000 words to this song alone, but draws no conclusions as to which version is 'correct'.
P. Stephenson, Buxton.

☐ THE song has been traced back to the conversion of England to Christianity and was probably an aid to teaching the Creed. There is a mystery about the symbols, as they draw on pagan as well as Hebraic/Christian imagery. A possible explanation would be: the lily-white boys are Christ and John the Baptist; the three rivals are the Magi; the six proud walkers are the water-pot bearers at the feast at Cana; the eight bold rangers (April-rainers?) could be the archangels; the five symbols at your door – possibly the Hebraic pentagon but more likely the five wounds of Christ; the nine bright shiners are possibly the nine joys of Mary; the seven stars in the sky are probably the Planets or perhaps the Great Bear.
Leon Bailey, Worcester.

☐ THE six proud walkers are the burghers of Calais, the rivals the three lovelies that poor Paris had to judge. The symbols at your door are the marks of lamb's blood on the entrances to the Hebrew homes in Egypt during the plagues – the first Passover.
Frances Nelson, Limekilns, Fife.

☐ IN *The White Goddess*, Chapter 10, Robert Graves equates the letters D and T (the 7th and 8th letters of the Beth-Luis-Nion tree alphabet) with the Lily White Boys. D is the sacred Druidic oak which rules the waxing year, and T is the evergreen oak or holly; the bloody oak which rules the waning part of the year. Jesus is often identified with the holly but it was not the holly king but the oak king who was crucified on a T-shaped cross. See also Sir Gawain and the Green Knight (oak and holly) who

agreed to behead each other each alternate New Year. (Midsummer and Midwinter).
Audrey Coleman, St Leonards on Sea, Sussex.

QUESTION: Twice I have had to exchange a compact disc because one band contained a kind of jamming noise. Can someone explain this?

☐ SIMPLE. The ability to track the optical information on a compact disc relies upon the laser beam actually 'reading' three tracks – the track that is reproducing the music at that instant, and those on either side: the track that has just been read and the one to follow. This operates what is called a servo mechanism, which keeps the reading head with absolute precision on the centre track. If the tracking mechanism momentarily fails to get the information off the disc – and this may be due to a disc fault (scratch or dirt) or a machine defect (get the lens cleaned) – then it sticks on the centre track. The disc is spinning at a few hundred times a second, the actual speed depending upon whether the disc is being 'read' on the outer or the inner tracks of the disc. The listener hears this track repeated at the same rate, hence the sound the questioner experiences.

Sometimes, cleaning the suspect disc gently with a soft cloth and isopropyl alcohol helps, but always clean round the disc; never across it. Even a finger mark can create this problem.
Reg Williamson, University of Keele.

QUESTION: What was the music played at Peter Sellers's funeral because he especially loathed it?

☐ IT WAS Glenn Miller's signature tune, 'In the Mood'. In Spike Milligan's war memoirs, it is explained that Sellers

grew to hate the song while working as a drummer in a dance band before the war. The tune was much requested, and so it was sometimes necessary to play it several times a night. Sellers was forced to listen to it to distraction, and so its playing at his memorial service was his private act of revenge.
Martin Locock, Walsall.

☐ MICHAEL Bentine gave a hilarious account of the service some time ago on television. Sellers had specifically requested that the music be played, but most people at the service, including the minister, did not realise that he detested the tune. The minister introduced it by saying that 'it was obviously a piece of music which meant a lot to Peter' and the mourners sat reverently listening to it. Bentine recounts that as one of the few people there who knew Sellers's real feelings about the piece he had great difficulty in not bursting out laughing.
John Irwin, Wilmslow, Cheshire.

☐ MARTIN Pocock's reply regarding Peter Sellers's funeral music was not strictly correct. 'In the Mood' was not Glen Miller's signature tune, but that of the British band leader, Joe Loss. Miller's signature tune was his own composition, 'Moonlight Serenade'.
Tony Voce, Eltham, London SE9.

QUESTION: In film studios' trademark logos, shown at the beginning of productions, (1) who was the Gainsborough lady? (2) what is the morse code message transmitted from the radio pylon in RKO Radio Pictures? and (3) why was the time changed from 8 o'clock to 11 o'clock on Big Ben in London Films?

☐ THE Gainsborough Lady was Glenys Lorimer. Her father was one of the Ostrer brothers who ran the studio.

She also appeared in several films. I knew her when I worked with London Film Productions in the Thirties.

My guess about the change of time on Big Ben is that, since the original was shot in black and white, it was shot a second time in colour, probably at the end of the Thirties.

Kay Mender, Todmorden, W. Yorks.

□ THE Morse code message transmitted from the radio pylon is – surprise, surprise – 'RKO Radio Pictures'.
George Greaves (ex-Leading Telegraphist Royal Navy), Hastings, E. Sussex.

QUESTION: What are the origins of the common surnames White, Black, Green and Brown? Why are there no Reds, Blues, Yellows, etc?

□ WITH the exception of yellow, all the colours may be found in one form or another today. Yellow seems to have fallen out of use quite early, though a Widow Yellowe of Suffolk was noted as late as 1674. Yellow's lack of favour might well be because of its pejorative meaning, 'cunning, duplicitous, hypocritical', which dates from as early as the fourteenth century. Among others in current use are: **Black** – Blache, Blatch, Black, Blake, Colley, Collie (coal black). **Blond** – Blunt, Blout, Blondel, Blundell. **Gold** – Golden, Goolden, Goulden. **Yellow** – Faugh (pale brown, reddish yellow), Favell (fallow or tawny), Flavell. **Red** – Read, Reed, Red, Rudd, Rous, Russell. **Sorrell** – (reddish brown), Soar, Sanguine, Sangwin. **Grey** – Gray, Grey, Hoar, Hore, Biss, Bissett, Grice, Griss, Girson, Grissom (grey hair). **Brown** – Brownett, Brunet, Brown, Dunn, Burnett, Burall, Borell, Nutbrown, Brownnutt, Brownutt, Brownhutt, Perbrun. **White** – White, Snow. **Blue** – Blewett, Bluett, and probably Blowe, Blaw. **Green** – Green.

As is obvious from the above, many of these colour-

names relate to hair colour or some other physical charac-
teristic like complexion or clothing. There are numerous
others which have Celtic origins, like the range of Welsh
names with derivatives of 'gwyn/gwen – white', usually in
the metaphorical sense of 'pure'.
*Derek Shields, Staffordshire Polytechnic, Stoke-on-
Trent.*

QUESTION: Can I, as an individual, nominate someone for a Nobel Prize?

☐ INDIVIDUALS in general cannot nominate someone for
a Nobel Prize. The rules vary from prize to prize but the
following examples can be given:

Literature: (1) Members of the Swedish Academy and
of other academies, institutions and societies similar to it
in membership and aims; (2) Professors of history of
literature or of languages at universities or university
colleges; (3) Nobel laureates in Literature; and (4) Presi-
dents of authors' organisations which are representative
of the literary activities of their respective countries.

Peace: (1) Active and former members of the Norwegian Nobel Committee and the advisers appointed by the
Norwegian Nobel Institute; (2) Members of the national
assemblies and governments of the different states and
members of the Interparliamentary Union; (3) Members
of the International Court of Arbitration at the Hague;
(4) Members of the Commission of the Permanent International Peace Bureau; (5) Members and associate
members of the Institut de Droit International; (6)
University professors of political science and jurispru-
dence, history and philosophy; and (7) Nobel Laureates
for Peace.
*Torsten Kälvemark, Cultural Attaché, Embassy of Swe-
den, London W1.*

QUESTION: In Chapter three of the sixth book of *The Return of the Native* by Thomas Hardy, Clym Yeobright is said to have resolved to become 'an itinerant preacher of the eleventh commandment'. To what does this refer?

☐ CHRIST gave the 'eleventh commandment' to his disciples at the Last Supper. It occurs in all the Gospels in different forms, but most succinctly in John 13, 34: 'Love one another; as I have loved you, that ye also love one another.'

Hardy's story refers in detail to several of the original 10 commandments. At the end of the novel, Clym Yeobright is following Christ just as the rich man was urged to do; he is nearly 33, has given up everything, and is seen preaching a Sermon on the Mount. Earlier (Book III, chapter 2) we have been told that 'Yeobright loved his kind' and a few lines later that 'he was ready at once to be the first unit sacrificed' – which is close to John's 'greater love hath no man than this, that a man lay down his life for his friends'.

In the same chapter Clym asks: 'Mother, what is "doing well"?', a question Hardy compares to Pilate's 'What is truth?'
Angela Costen, Axbridge, Somerset.

☐ I KNOW nothing of the preachings of Clym Yeobright, but surely the eleventh commandment has always been 'Thou shalt not be found out.' Certainly it was when I was at school.
Pat Paget, Manchester 20.

QUESTION: Was King Charles I really the shortest British monarch at 4ft 7in?

☐ ACCORDING to the omniscient Monty Python, 'The

most interesting thing about King Charles I is that he was
5ft 6in tall at the start of his reign, but only 4ft 8in tall at
the end of it.'
Adele Barnett, Devizes.

**QUESTION: Did the Man Who Broke the Bank at
Monte Carlo really exist, and if so, what was his
name?**

☐ HE was a shady American confidence-trickster called
Charles Deville Wells, who turned $400 into $40,000 in
three days. His example inspired many, but more
gamblers committed suicide at Monte Carlo than made
earnings on this scale. For more information see my
Guide to Provence (Penguin, 1989).
Michael Jacobs, London E9.

☐ HE was Joseph Hobson Jagger whose story is told in
David James's *Victorian Bradford: The Living Past.* Jagger was an engineer who worked at Buttershaw Mill and
when he visited Monte Carlo in 1875 he analysed the
gearing of the roulette wheel in the casino and proceeded
to win two million francs in eight days. Subsequently,
Frederick Gilbert, on hearing of Jagger's exploits wrote
the famous song ' The Man Who Broke the Bank at Monte
Carlo.'
David M. Kennedy, Ilkley, Yorks.

**QUESTION: Which books were removed from the
New Testament in AD 367 by Athanasius of Alexandria, in AD 393 by the Council of Hippo and in AD 397
by the Council of Carthage?**

☐ IT IS misleading to talk of books being 'removed' from
the New Testament; not until well into the fourth century
AD was there agreement on what the canon of the New

Testament actually was. This came about after a long and gradual process, and was in the form of an accepted consensus rather than a formal statement. In fact, no Ecumenical Council ever made a definitive pronouncement on the subject, reflecting the fact that this was one issue in the early church which was singularly free of controversy.

Before this time, various lists of books had been in circulation in different areas. From these we can identify five principal 'fringe' books later omitted from the canon proper. They are: the Didache (or Teaching of the Twelve Apostles), the Shepherd of Hermas, the Apocalypse of Peter, the Epistle of Barnabas and the Epistle of Clement. Their eventual exclusion was not because they were regarded as heretical, but because they either lacked apostolic authorship or were thought to be too shallow in spiritual content.

Athanasius, in his Easter Letter of AD 367, set out his list of books which were to be regarded as Scripture. His is the earliest extant list which corresponds with the canon of the New Testament as we now know it.

In addition, he states that the Didache and the Shepherd, while not to be regarded on this level, were still worthy of study by catechumens. The respect Athanasius commanded was such that his list was accepted in Rome in AD 383, and adopted by the Council of Carthage in AD 397.

The Council of Hippo in AD 393 was more concerned with the status of the Old Testament Apocrypha, and appears not to have discussed the canon of the New Testament at any length. The Athanasian canon thus came to be gradually accepted throughout the church.

M. R. James, of ghost story fame, published a translation of all the significant post-apostolic writings in 1924, which is still in print *(The Apocryphal New Testament, Oxford University Press)*.
Alan M. Linfield, Tring, Herts.

QUESTION: In the 1950s many of us had a ginger beer plant. How is this plant made and how does one use it to make ginger beer?

☐ PUT 2oz baker's yeast or ½oz dried yeast in a large glass jar and add ½pint tepid water, 2 level teaspoons each of sugar and ground ginger. When stirred, it will begin to froth. Daily, for a week, feed the plant with 1 teaspoon each of sugar and ginger.

At the end of a week, strain the liquid carefully through muslin, retaining the residue, and add the juice of 2 lemons, 1lb sugar and 2 pints of warm water. Stir mixture well to dissolve sugar. Bottle when cool.

This is where your neighbour comes in: divide the residue into two, keeping one part and giving (or throwing) the other away. Place your half of the plant into a large jar and carry out the process again, but this time leaving out the yeast.

The plant won't live for more than a week or ten days unless it is rejuvenated and started again. The ginger beer, by the way, is ready to drink in another week's time, but cork it lightly at first, and serve chilled.
Mike Whitley, Whitstable, Kent.

☐ I AM bothered by Mike Whitley's recipe for ginger beer, which includes the instruction to add 1lb of sugar and two pints of water before bottling. I hope that anyone who gets to that stage will realise that this is far too high a concentration of sugar − from the point of view of taste, and, more importantly, for safety. One half teaspoon per pint is enough to produce a fizz in the bottle; more than that is likely to be explosive. It's also very important to use sound glass bottles, able to withstand pressure − preferably beer or cider bottles with crown caps or screw tops.
(Dr) Andrew Collins, Aberdeen.

☐ THE recipe for ginger beer lacks one vital sentence.

After straining the liquid and adding the juice of 2 lemons, 1lb sugar and 2pts *boiling* water, the volume should be made up to one gallon with cold water before bottling.
Elizabeth Hird, Kelso.

QUESTION: Who lives at No 9 Downing Street?

☐ NOBODY lives at No 9, but there is a door that goes into the Privy Council building from Downing Street. It is not well marked and is secluded from the view of anybody standing at the palatial gates at the bottom of Downing Street.
Lawrence Brennan, Ampleforth College, York.

QUESTION: Why do television weather forecasters stand to the left of the screen? Most of our weather comes from the west, which means that we can only with difficulty see the storms that are coming.

☐ WEATHERFOLK stand on the left as we have fewer viewers over the Atlantic than East Anglia. If there is anything big behind us we do a little jig.

A high proportion of weathermen have been left-handed, by the way. We are not sure if this is Darwinism (clever left hand gets the job) or if left-handers have the sort of twisted mind which is happy with this four-dimensional task.

Anyway, it's probably all the other way round in Japan.
Ian McCaskill, BBC Weatherman, London W12.

☐ THE right and top of the screen is the dominant and natural place for the eye first to start in a scan of the screen. Consequently the map is placed there, providing the necessary instant visual information. The forecaster

and his words are secondary, so he is placed on the left, the final resting place for the eye.
Sian Griffith, Liverpool 37.

QUESTION: Why does eating cheese last thing at night give you nightmares?

☐ FOR anyone with an interest in psycho-analysis this question is a dream. And especially for the Post-Freudians to whom nightmares (or nocturnal horses as they are known in the trade) are a piece of cake. Basically it's horses for courses and, as we all know, the traditional English supper finishes with cheese.
(Dr) Jim Watters, Editor, Tavistock Gazette, *London NW3.*

☐ I UNDERSTAND that cheese contains a larger than average amount of a chemical called 'tyramine', which is a sympathomimetic agent (i.e. affecting that part of the nervous system which responds to 'fight, flight and panic'). Its effects seem to be predominantly on the brain, and for this reason it may give some people headaches.
Paul Humber, Brasted, Kent.

QUESTION: Trivial Pursuit tells us that Charles Lindbergh took four sandwiches on his record-breaking transatlantic flight. What was in them?

☐ THEY had a meat filling, but Lindbergh's own account of the flight, *Spirit of St Louis* (Tandem, 1975) doesn't say which kind. In fact there were *five* sandwiches, of which only one was eaten on the flight, over France. Lindbergh considered throwing the wrapper out of the window, but decided he didn't want 'the litter from a sandwich to symbolise my first contact with France'.

As well as the butties he carried five quarts of water and five 8oz cans of army rations in case of a forced landing. *Katharine Jeffery, Bath.*

QUESTION: What is the logic (or madness) behind the postal districts of London? Why, for example, is N1 next to N7? And is there an SE2?

☐ THE numbering of London's postal districts is not as illogical as it at first appears.

In 1856 London was divided into 10 postal districts: EC; E; WC; W; N; NW; SE; SW; S; NE, of which the last two were dropped within a few years.

In 1917, numbered districts were introduced, the 1s and central districts corresponding with the original divisions, and the additional districts from two onwards in

alphabetical order (with a few irregularities), e.g. N2 – East Finchley; N3 – Finchley; N4 Finsbury Park; N5 – Highbury; N6 – Highgate; N7 Holloway and so on. And yes, there is an SE2 – covering Abbey Wood.
Marye Wyvill, London NW5.

QUESTION: Which musicians played the repeated jazz theme on the soundtrack of *M Hulot's Holiday*, and does it have a title?

☐ THE tune is 'Quel Temps Fait-il à Paris?' written by Alain Romans and played by Jean Yatove's orchestra. It was included on a 1968 Philips LP (SBL 7858) of music from five Tati films.
Tony Augarde, Oxford.

QUESTION: What is the origin of 'The show's not over till the fat lady sings'?

☐ THE quote is, I believe, 'The game isn't over until the fat lady sings.' It comes from American baseball. At the end of a game a diva – often of Rubenesque physique – would sing The Star-Spangled Banner.
David Aiken, Southall, Middx.

☐ I THINK David Aiken is wrong. The American national anthem invariably precedes a baseball game, and may be sung by almost anyone, male or female, fat or thin. According to the Library of Congress book, *Respectfully Quoted*, published last year, the phrase 'the opera ain't over till the fat lady sings' was coined in 1978 by Dan Cook, a sports writer from San Antonio, Texas, after his town's basketball team had gone one up in a championship series. He meant it as a warning, and the phrase was later popularised by the coach of the team which finally

did win the series. That team was Washington, which may be why the saying entered American political jargon. It seems to reflect no more than a layman's vague idea of what happens at an opera. There is a baseball connection, however. During the worst point of their dreadful 1988 season, the Baltimore Orioles club had posters put up around the city showing an immense diva with spear and Viking helmet, and a slogan saying, 'She ain't sung yet.'
Simon Hoggart, Twickenham.

QUESTION: Who were Tam o' Shanter and Souter Johnny?

□ TAM o' Shanter, the hero of Burns's poem of that name, was most probably based on Douglas Graham (1739-1811), tenant of the farm of Shanter on Ayrshire's Carrick coast. He owned a boat which he called *Tam o' Shanter* and was known over a wide area for his convivial habits. Souter Johnie, his 'ancient, trusty, drouthy cronie' is a more doubtful figure, though he may have been John Davidson (1723-1806), who was a souter (shoemaker) living nearby.

When Tam's name is run together in our Scottish way of speaking it sounds like 'tammishanter', so Burns may have intended a pun: 'mishanter' is a Laalans word for a mishap or disaster. Notice that the hero is Tam o' Shanter – Tom of the farm of that name. There is no surname O'Shanter. Burns spells Johnny as Johnie.

For further information see volume 1 of the Centenary Edition of the poetry of Robert Burns, edited by W. E. Henley and T. F. Henderson, 4 vols, Edinburgh, 1896.
Seumas Stewart, Chipping Campden, Glos.

□ SOUTER Johnny (John Davidson) was my great, great, great grandfather. He was born in Kirkoswald and his gravestone stands in the churchyard there.
(Mrs) A. K. Riley, Milngavie, Glasgow.

QUESTION: Who originally made the remark, 'I have seen the future and it works'?

☐ ACCORDING to William C. Bullitt, a 28-year-old information attaché with the American mission to Russia, this celebrated mantra was 'finally perfected' on a train to Stockholm in February 1919, by his travelling companion, 51-year-old American journalist Lincoln Steffens, a known Bolshevik sympathiser and publicist.

Days before they even made their first contact with Bolshevik agents and set out together for the Russian frontier, Steffens was working feverishly on a one-line telegram that would 'electrify the world'. It began as 'I have been over into the future and it works' – by which he meant, in part, that the Bolsheviks were not a bad dream but real and there to stay. In its perfected form – 'I have seen the future and it works' – it would ring in Western ears for the next two decades.
Ray Boston, Cardiff.

☐ IT IS also worth noting John Cole's comment on the then up-and-coming Kenneth Baker, MP: 'I have seen the future and it smirks.'
Jerry Strachan, Middlesborough, Cleveland.

QUESTION: Why do washing machines prevent you from opening the door for several minutes after the washing cycle finishes?

☐ TERTIARY safety. Primary safety would stop the drum before the door opens. Secondary safety would prevent your hand being put into the drum if it hadn't stopped. Tertiary safety is the prevention of law suits against the manufacturer.

The cheapest way of achieving this is to make millions of housewives wait many millions of minutes, a monumental waste of time, by using the cheapest possible gadget, a heated strip of bendy metal which takes a long time to cool down and unbend.

W. D. Brinicombe, Ealing, London W5.

QUESTION: The lovely smell of rain on hot dried earth: what are we actually smelling?

☐ THIS earthy odour is chiefly that of chemicals, notably geosmins, produced by a particular group of soil bacteria, the filamentous streptomycetes. These microbes are famous for producing unusual chemicals, and are the source of many antibiotics, such as streptomycin. The occurrence of the geosmin smell after rain is presumably due to displacement of the volatile chemical from the air spaces between the soil particles.

(Prof.) Graham Gooday, Dept of Molecular and Cell Biology, University of Aberdeen.

☐ PROFESSOR Gooday's explanation of soil bacteria producing chemicals is perhaps not the only cause of the smell. In the field, we geologists often breathe gently on newly-prised-out rock specimens as a rough guide to which are arenaceous (sandstones, etc) or argillaceous (clay-like, mudstones and so on).

The argillaceous rocks smell very much like rain on hot earth. Dana's *Textbook of Mineralogy* notes that the smell is 'obtained from serpentine and some allied minerals, after moistening them with the breath'.

Arenaceous rocks, being mostly silica, have little or no smell.

Len Clarke, Uxbridge, Middx.

QUESTION: Why are snooker tables green?

□ ACCORDING to the *Hamlyn Encyclopaedia of Snooker* the game was originally played on grass (?!) 'so when the game was brought indoors and played on a table, the green cloth was used so as to make the playing surface look like grass'.
Terry Edwards, London E1.

□ THE manufacture of snooker tables in standard green stems from a decision in Plymouth Petty sessions on 8 December, 1871. Before then tables had been made in a variety of colours but were most often orange. In the poor lighting of the day it was difficult to see the exact movements of the ball against the table. This often gave rise to disagreements and disputes between players. In the case before the court Arthur Terry, a marine, was charged with 'occasioning violent harm to one Riland Metcalfe in the course of a melée which ensued between them following a dispute regarding movement of the balls in a game of "the snooker" '.

Terry was found guilty but allowed to leave the court unpunished because in the opinion of the magistrate 'Terry was not of full blame, the colour of the table being in part at fault.' The magistrate then recommended that 'henceforth the cause of harmonious play would be advanced if the snooker tables were manufactured in standard green, giving strong contrast to the red of the ball'.
G. A. Ilbert, Plymouth.

QUESTION: Why is it that in all the televised sports only soccer players spit?

□ IN aerobic activity participants build up much more spittle and mucus than in normal activity. The question is

THERE IS SOME CORNER OF A FOREIGN FIELD.

how to get rid of this. There are two options, spit it out or swallow it.

Tennis players usually opt to swallow it with a little drink when changing ends (although I've seen spitting tennis players before now). Snooker and darts players don't usually have the need to.

Perhaps cricketers are not seen spitting on television because the players are spread so thinly over the ground and there is so much 'non-active' time that it is statistically improbable that a spitting player would be caught on television.

It would be detrimental for squash players to spit on the floor as they may slip on it later (but they do wipe their sweat all over the walls).

But perhaps the biggest reason for catching football

players spitting on TV is the style of coverage, i.e. high-lighting, with a close-up, the player who has just made a long sprint to score a goal.
Stephen Bloyce, Leeds.

□ IAN Botham is a frequent spitter on camera, and Steve Ovett actually blew his nose with his fingers once on TV. I gave up fun runs because there were so many people spitting over their shoulders. Guess who was behind!
G. L. Bennett, Herne Bay, Kent.

□ IT SEEMS to be a way of affirming masculinity, and may be a very primitive remnant of marking territory – something akin to dogs urinating.
Philip Millard, Almondsbury, Bristol, Avon.

QUESTION: Israel is not in Europe, so why is it allowed to enter the Eurovision Song Contest?

□ ISRAEL is entitled to enter since it has long been a member of Eurovision – the principal criterion for taking part. The country's television service was established under the guidance of European experts including Stuart Hood of the BBC.

Israel is also a member of the European Broadcasting Union. It won the song contest in 1978 and again in 1979, when it was televised from Jerusalem. Having won for the second time it had the right to host the competition again in 1980, but handed this to Holland due to lack of funds.
Rodney Greenberg, High Wycombe, Bucks.

□ IN the past Morocco has entered, and Libya could if it wished as well, as both have European Broadcasting Union status.
Liam Jarnecki, London E15.

□ THE right to participate in the contest is contingent on membership of the European Broadcasting Union. The statutes of the Union limit membership 'primarily ... to organisations in the European Broadcasting Area. This area, as defined by the International Telecommunications Union, extends from the Atlantic to the meridian 40°E. It is bounded on the south by the 30th parallel.' Jerusalem, the official headquarters of Israeli Television, is 35°E, and on the 32nd parallel.

This definition also allows for participation by Algeria, Egypt, Jordan, the Lebanon, Libya, Morocco, Syria and Tunisia. Israeli participation deters these countries on a point of principle, although Morocco did enter in 1980 when Israel withdrew for Passover. Samira Bensaid sang 'Betakit Hob', a plea for racial harmony based on the distressing observation that, 'whilst our skins may be different colours, we are all red on the inside'. It came second from last and Morocco has not repeated the experiment.

The only country ever refused entry to the contest is Liechtenstein, turned down in 1976 on the harsh grounds that it had no television station or transmission facilities of any sort. In a compromise to avert a diplomatic incident, Swiss Television agreed that their entry be officially that of 'The Swiss Confederation and Liechtenstein'; this is a nice point, since the full name won't fit on the scoreboard.

A further complication is that of Eastern Europe. Yugoslavia has always been a member of Eurovision; indeed, Croatian television staged the contest this year in Zagreb following their famous 1989 victory with 'Rock Me, Baby'. The other countries of Eastern Europe — except Albania — have a parallel organisation called Intervision, with its own song contest. In the state of flux now characterising the old structures of Europe, these countries may be expected to avail themselves of Eurovision membership, thereby increasing the length of the contest by about an hour and causing terminal seizure of the voting system. Gorbachev has a lot to answer for.
Andrew Latto, Thornton Heath, Surrey.

QUESTION: If any number multiplied by zero is zero, and any number divided by itself is one, and any number divided by zero is infinity, what is zero divided by zero?

☐ Zero divided by zero is quite indeterminate. For if A is B times C, then A divided by B is C. But zero is equal to zero times any number whatever. Therefore zero divided by zero is any number whatever.
Ivor Etherington, Easdale, Argyll.

QUESTION: Why were the British known as gringos in South America?

☐ Americans from the United States are gringos, the British are gringitos (i.e. little gringos). The term is said to originate from the Mexicans mishearing invading US soldiers singing 'Green Grow the Rushes-O' during the 1846-48 war between their countries.

It is appropriate that the first major act of US aggression in its so-called backyard should have engendered a fine Spanish term of racial abuse that remains current to this day.
Ralph Lloyd-Jones, London SE22.

☐ The problem with the answer that 'gringo' came from the song, 'Green Grow the Rushes-O', sung during the 1846-48 war between Mexico and the US, is that 'gringo' is attested to in a Castilian dictionary of 1787, which defines it as the name given in Malaga to foreigners with thick accents whose Spanish is difficult to understand. In Madrid it especially referred to the Irish. This Spanish 'gringo', which was exported to Mexico, comes from the 'Griego' (Greek) and meant that the speech of foreigners sounded unintelligible. Greek has since medieval times had a reputation for unintelligibility.
Jack Griffiths, Ferring, W. Sussex.

QUESTION: Why did the builders of the classical Greek temples make their columns fluted? When did they begin fluting and how did they do it with such mathematical precision?

☐ CLASSICAL Greek temple columns were fluted because they were derived from timber construction. The columns are a stone form of a tree trunk debarked with an adze. In fact the whole of the Doric order has been described as a 'carpentry in marble' (Bannister Fletcher, *A History of Architecture*) and can be understood as timber construction.

Timber became stone around 600 BC but similar fluting occurs in columns in the tombs at Beni Hasan in Egypt, dated 2130-1786 BC. The mathematical precision of the work would need a master mason to describe the process but would have been simple to masons who introduced subtle optical corrections to classical temple architecture to offset optical distortion. I would like to know how they did it, too .

This is not the only example of the translation of one technique into another material. There are Egyptian lotus columns where the rope binding and timber wedges are faithfully reproduced, as are the plant forms.
Ian Pickering, The Mackintosh School of Architecture, Glasgow.

QUESTION: Does scratching your head really help?

☐ INDEED it does. While contemplating the action of scratching your head, your sub-conscious mind has time to insert an answer into your conscious mind and bingo – the solution appears. For more profound problems either brew tea and/or raise the Titanic.
Zina Kaye, London SW6.

☐ I SCRATCHED my way through eight O-levels and passed only three of them. The answer is no.
C. Leach, Cambridge.

☐ ANIMAL behaviourists have guessed this to be a form of displacement activity: 'inappropriate' behaviour following indecision or conflicting interests. Another example is the stickleback at the edge of its territory. Torn between pursuit and defence, it stands on its head.
R. B. Taylor, London SW19.

QUESTION: Where was the first banana republic, and who named it so?

☐ A BANANA republic is a politically unstable country, with an economy dependent on one or two products, such as bananas. Furthermore, this sector is dominated by one or two companies, usually foreign-owned. The classic banana republic is Honduras, which was, from the 1880s, dominated by the American-owned United Fruit and Standard Fruit companies, whose banana exports provided the republic's foreign earnings.

One reluctant American expatriate in Honduras was O. Henry, the short story writer, fleeing from the law. He spent a year there, during which time he coined the phrase 'banana republic'. However, Honduras was not the original republic to grow bananas, which had been introduced to the Canaries and West Indies many years before.
R. L. Vickers, Crewe, Cheshire.

☐ THE term is bit of a misnomer, as two of the so-called banana republics, Nicaragua and El Salvador, produce very few, if any, bananas.
Siobhan Kenny, Glasgow.

QUESTION: What is the origin of that maddening rhythm, 'Pom tiddly-om-pom pom-pom'?

☐ ACCORDING to *The Book of World-Famous Music* by James J. Fuld, the phrase first occurs in 'Hot Scotch Rag' by H. A. Fischlet (1911). It was later used in several songs, with a variety of words added. One possible forerunner is Sullivan's setting of the words 'Shall they stoop to insult? No! No!' in *HMS Pinafore* (1878). After several bars of austere harmony, the last two words are preceded by an open octave played by a full orchestra – a strikingly bathetic cadence.

Tom McCanna, Dept of Music, University of Sheffield.

☐ THE origin is said to be the sound of the coaches of the Chicago elevated railway (the El') running on the overhead track. Even more maddeningly they say 'shave 'n a haircut, two bits'.

(Professor) Robert Moore, Holywell, Clwyd.

QUESTION: During an orchestral concert, why do string players find it necessary to re-tune their instruments at each interval? Does this mean they have been out of tune when playing the preceding music?

☐ THE strings on these instruments are all under tension, which will lessen as the instruments are played. If the concert hall gets warmer as the concert goes on, the strings will tend to expand slightly, which will also decrease their tension. The result is that the tuning of the strings gets somewhat flatter as the piece proceeds. The competent player can compensate for this during a single movement and so avoid playing out of tune, but may well wish to check the tuning between separate items. I sus-

pect also that this re-tuning helps relieve nervous tension.
Wind players have the opposite problem as their instruments tend to sharpen as the programme proceeds, especially if the venue gets warmer. So they may also wish to
re-tune between movements and certainly between individual items.

(Rev.) Harold Webb, Guildford, Surrey.

**QUESTION: By what method did the Greek astro-
nomer, Aristarchus of Samos, make a remarkably
accurate measurement of the earth's circumference
in roughly 250 BC ?**

☐ I THINK your questioner has his Greeks in a twist.
Aristarchus of Samos is now best known for his anticipa-
tion of Copernicus' heliocentric (sun-centred) cosmology
rather than for measuring the circumference of the earth,
though he did estimate the distances to, and sizes of, the
sun and moon – alas, rather inaccurately! The first
circumference measurement of which we have a reasonably full account is the one made by Eratosthenes, librarian at Alexandria, sometime during the third century BC.
He measured the angle between the rays of the midday
sun and a vertical post in Alexandria on a day when the
sun was directly overhead at Syene (near Aswan), 5,000
'stades' due south of Alexandria, and found the angle to
be (about) a fiftieth of a full circle (7½ degrees). If 5,000
stades corresponds to a fiftieth of the circumference, then
the whole circumference must be (5,000:50), or 250,000
stades. Unfortunately, the figures we have are rounded,
and we do not know the exact length of his unit, the stade.
However, modern consensus suggests that his figure was
probably a few per cent low – still, not bad for an
astronomical measurement made with a stick.

Steve Cook, Nottingham.

QUESTION: Why are some motorway surfaces concrete while others are tarmac?

☐ TARMAC is a misnomer. The surfacing layer is hot rolled asphalt laid on a stone base. This is known as 'flexible' construction, whereas concrete slabbing is a 'rigid' design. Many factors are involved in the comparison of the two methods – among these are the nature of the subsoil, the surface riding qualities and availability of the various materials near the construction site. In theory, concrete motorways should require only minimal maintenance but in practice, for various reasons, they often incur considerable post-construction costs. Asphalt surfaces must be totally renewed at intervals of perhaps 10 to 20 years. Motorway contractors are very often given the option at tender stage between rigid and flexible construction and the eventual choice by the authority concerned is based only on economics.
L. E. Schraer, Steyning, W. Sussex.

☐ WHEN I protested about the high level of noise produced by the concrete section of the M25 I was told by the Department of Transport that there was a very strong concrete lobby and there was an unwritten agreement that the cement companies should get a fair share of all motorway construction. I was assured that the cost of laying and maintaining concrete was no higher than tarmac. The one snag is that the concrete has to be heavily serrated to stop skidding and this causes the high-pitched whine.
H. M. Longworth, Upminster, Essex.

QUESTION: What is the reason for the little white square in the top right-hand corner of the picture on a TV screen? Why does it appear and disappear?

☐ THE dot is seen on ITV and Channel Four. It alerts the 15 regional ITV companies to get ready to play in the commercials on both networks. It appears about a minute before the break, and disappears with five seconds to go. *Steve Perkins, Regional Officer, Independent Broadcasting Authority, Norwich.*

☐ IT IS known in the trade as a 'cue dot'. When it appears, it signifies 30 seconds before the next programme. It disappears at 10 seconds to go. It is vital for getting the following programme on air on time – and without gaps in between. For BBC employees in Birmingham, it is London's sign (for that is where it originates) to us to wake up.
Jane McLean, Production Assistant, BBC, Birmingham 5.

QUESTION: Why did Harry S. Truman change his middle name to just S?

☐ ROY Jenkins, in his excellent biography of Truman, tells us that 'the S stood for nothing but S'. By way of explanation, he adds that the choice of form by Truman's parents stemmed from a desire to balance between the competing claims of Soloman Young (Truman's maternal grandfather) and Anderson Shippe Truman (his paternal grandfather). Whether either was satisfied, Jenkins adds, is not recorded. Truman was, therefore, born and registered as Harry S. Truman at Lamar, Barton County, Missouri on 8 May, 1884. I do not know if it is permitted to ask a question when giving an answer, but where did the story about Sergei originate from?
T. D. Rees, Gosport, Hants.

QUESTION: Where does the expression 'Holy Mackerel' come from?

☐ JESUS fed the five thousand with mackerel. Indentations either side of the fish's head show where it was held by Jesus.
Alec Shannon, Bitton, Bristol.

☐ THE phrase is connected with Sunday trading laws, as fish could not be sold at Sunday markets. However, the flesh of a mackerel deteriorates very quickly once caught, and so mackerel were exempt from the law.
Mike Ferdinands, Leeds.

QUESTION: Why must the letter Q always be followed by U in English?

☐ THE first European alphabet was Greek, which was an

adaptation of Old Phoenician. This contained the letters gamma (T or G), kappa (K) and qoppa (Q). These last two represent the 'K' sounds in 'keep' and 'coop' which the early Semites distinguished (and I believe some of their descendants still do). The Greeks made no such distinction and soon dropped the Q. Before they did, the Etruscans took over the alphabet. The Etruscans had no 'G' sound in their language, so they used the gamma as yet another 'K'. The gamma, which by now looked less like an inverted L and more like a C, was used before E and I; the kappa before A and the qoppa before U and O. This is why the letters are called cee, kay and quoo. The Romans took over the Etruscan alphabet and had to re-invent a 'G' letter by adding a small stoke to the C. They eventually dropped the K, using the C before all vowels except U, which is still the case today. Contact with Greece and the introduction of Greek loan words made it necessary to reintroduce the K at a later date.

John Ward, Knowle, Bristol.

□ SIMON McCARTIN was a bit too *qick* with his *qestion*, and my *qery* is how can he pronounce these words without pronouncing the essential 'U'? Until we have a symbol for a combined consonant and vowel, we can only continue to use two such. Now perhaps he can tell us *hwy* he did not ask *hwat* is the reason for spelling *'hwich'* as we do, and *hwen* it started?

W. W. Bloomfield, Camberley, Surrey.

QUESTION: Why did the illustrator, Ernest Shepard, get his animals mixed up in his illustration on page 30 of the original *Wind in the Willows*? Who changed them around in later editions?

□ IN the early 1950s I had just become production manager of Methuen, the publishers of *Wind in the*

The Wind in the Willows:
(LEFT: *original illustration*, RIGHT: *revised version*)

Willows, when we received a letter, penned in an uncertain, childish hand on a piece of green ruled paper with not a single square edge to it, which pointed out that one of Shepard's famous illustrations showed 'Ratty rowing the boat and Mole as passenger, when it ought to have been the other way round!'

The little boy was absolutely right. Some 60 impressions of the classic had contained an incorrect illustration and no one had previously pointed it out. Regrettably for posterity, the observant correspondent had forgotten to include his address on the letter so we were never able to thank him. It fell to me to write to Shepard, who was still going strong in those days, to explain the situation. Almost by return of post I received a new drawing, now correct in detail, and otherwise virtually a facsimile of the other one in that every apparently careless line of his seemingly rather free-style drawing was precisely where it had been in the first version.

It was the beginning of a long and close friendship with Shepard, who was known to his friends as 'Kipper', and I eventually persuaded him to produce colour plates for A.

A. Milne's Pooh books and *The World of Christopher Robin*, and, indeed, for *Wind in the Willows*.
Frank Herrmann, Maldon, Essex.

QUESTION: Did Adolf Hitler ever visit Liverpool, and if so, why?

□ THE story rests on the authority of his sister-in-law, Bridget. In a manuscript written in the 1930s, she claims that Hitler arrived in the city in November 1912 in order to stay with his half-brother, Alois, who lived in Upper Stanhope Street. Hitler remained for several months and Robert Payne (who recounts the story in *The Life and Death of Adolf Hitler*) speculates that the motive behind his visit was a desire to evade the Austrian authorities, who were hunting him because of his failure to register for military service.

There is no other evidence for this episode in Hitler's life; Bridget wrote the manuscript when he was at the height of his power and, in the absence of any independent confirmation of the story, the suspicion must be that it was fabricated in order to cash in on her brother-in-law's fame.
P. M. Ray, Harrogate, N. Yorks.

□ READ *The Memoirs of Bridget Hitler*, edited by Michael Unger, published by Duckworth in 1979 at £4.95.
Alan Love, Pidley, Cambs.

□ THE Liverpool ice rink in Wavertree, for some perverse reason, kept a pair of his skating boots on display behind a glass panel.
(Miss) M. Summers, Liverpool 4.

□ HE went to Liverpool to study art.
B. G. Hughes, Liverpool 23.

☐ APPARENTLY he spent his time watching the flow of sea traffic from the docks. Perhaps dreaming of empires?
Jane Speare, Alton, Hants.

☐ ANOTHER rumour was that Haile Selassie, the Lion of Juda and Emperor of Ethiopia, spent the years of the Second World War in exile in Liverpool, in Alexandra Drive. Two golden-coloured lion statues were supposed to mark the house as recently as the 1970s, and the only Italian plane to bomb Britain was said to have dropped its load on Liverpool in an attempt to get the Emperor.

What is undoubtedly true, but perhaps of interest only to a minority, is that Michael Bakunin, the noted Russian anarchist, and serious rival to Marx as an international revolutionary in the nineteenth century, passed through Liverpool on his epic escape from Siberia via Vladivostok, Yokohama, San Francisco, New York and London. He disembarked from a transatlantic liner at Liverpool, and took the train from Lime Street station to London.
(Dr) Moss Madden, Liverpool.

QUESTION: Who first gave the command, 'Home, James, and don't spare the horses'?

☐ THE preface to the first (1941) edition of the *Oxford Dictionary of Quotations*, and reproduced in the current third edition, states: 'Some quotations have had to be omitted because every effort to trace the source has failed, e.g. "Home, James, and don't spare the horses".' So bonus points for anyone who comes up with the answer to this one.
John Swan, Whitley Bay, Tyne and Wear.

☐ 'HOME, James, and don't spare the horses (This night has been ruin to me)' was a song recorded by Elsie Carlyle, with Ambrose and his orchestra, in 1934. It was

written by Fred Hillebrand, the American composer of another song which failed to get into the *Oxford Dictionary of Quotations*, 'The Time Is Not Propitious, Aloysius'.
Denis Norden, London W1.

QUESTION: What do the letters TOG stand for when used to specify the warmth factor of duvets?

☐ THE letters do not stand for anything: the tog is the British unit of clothing insulation (I have always assumed it to be an analogue, in origin, of usages such as 'sports togs', commonly used by schoolboys of mine and earlier generations). Physically, 1 tog is a thermal resistance of $0.1 \text{ m}^{K/W}$. The brand leader, i.e. the international unit, is the clo, unleashed upon an unsuspecting world in 1941 by the remarkably named Professor A. Pharo Gagge of New Haven, Connecticut. This is defined as the thermal insulation required to keep a sedentary person comfortable at 21°C, i.e. $0.155 \text{ m}^2\text{K/W}$. Thus, the tog is 0.645 of a clo.
I. D. Griffiths, University of Surrey, Guildford.

QUESTION: Why do opinion polls ask 'If there were a general election tomorrow ... ', etc, instead of 'today' or 'next Thursday' (which is usually the case)?

☐ IN the monthly polls between elections we ask 'tomorrow' to avoid people saying in response 'It depends.' When an election is called, we shift the question wording to suit, e.g. 'As you may know, there are local council elections in many areas on Thursday, 3 May. How likely is it that you will get along to vote in these council elections?' (Asked of those where local elections are being

held.) Then (asked of those intending to vote): 'If you do get along to vote, which party will you vote for?'
Bob Worcester, Mori, London SW1.

QUESTION: Why are pale flowers commoner in spring than summer?

☐ SPRING flowers such as primroses are pale in colour because these colours show up well in twilight when moths are feeding. Many spring flowers are pollinated by moths. The brighter colours of summer flowers attract day-feeding insects like bees.
Pat McLaren, Bishopston, Bristol.

☐ I DON'T think your correspondent gave the full answer. It has been shown that by feeding bees on differently coloured plates that they have a slightly different range of colour vision from us. They have very poor visual discrimination at the red–yellow end of the spectrum but are particularly sensitive to colours in the blue–purple range. They can also see ultra-violet and many flowers which appear red or yellow to us have been shown to emit strong ultra-violet signals to bees. Many spring flowers that are yellow or white are bulbs or corms which can multiply by vegetative means (i.e. increasing the number of bulbs) and have less need to attract insects.
(Mrs) Anne Fraser, Fishponds, Bristol.

QUESTION: Do the living now outnumber the dead?

☐ THE answer is no; the living population forms about 9 per cent of the total population who have ever lived, so the dead outnumber the living by about ten to one.
John Haskey, Statistician, Office of Population Studies, London.

QUESTION: Do dock leaves alleviate nettle stings?

☐ YES, it is absolutely true that dock leaves alleviate nettle stings and fortunately the two plants are generally found close to each other. As a life-long walker of country by-ways, I have personal knowledge that a dock leaf wrapped around a nettle sting instantly cools and soothes the pain and inflammation. Gail Duff, in her excellent book, *Country Wisdom* (Pan), states: 'Rub nettle stings with a dock leaf – it never fails to work, even if the stings are severe.' She adds a charm to repeat at the same time:

>Nettle out, dock in,
>Dock remove nettle sting,
>In dock, out nettle,
>Don't let the blood settle.

Thus, no doubt, producing a beneficial psychological effect.

Hilda Williams, Gillingham, Kent.

QUESTION: Why do slugs die when they come into contact with salt?

☐ THE slug has a moist skin, so when you sprinkle salt on to it a strong brine quickly forms. The process of osmosis then begins, by which water is drawn from a weak solution (in this case the body fluid of the slug) into a stronger one. Result: the slug dies a lingering death by dehydration. Gardeners may believe this is just retribution for the damage the small creatures wreak on their lettuces, but salt could do your garden more harm than the slugs. A quicker and kinder method, which my father uses, is to drop them into a pan of very hot water, where they die instantly and are ultimately recycled on a compost heap.

Dave Headey, Farringdon, Oxon.

QUESTION: Why is it that when you see a person yawn you want to yawn yourself?

□ THE function of yawning is poorly understood. It is a common behaviour in a wide range of animals but contagious yawning has been observed only in humans. One hypothesis is that in humans yawning has a paralinguistic function in communicating the subject's state of wakefulness to other members of his social group. According to this hypothesis, yawning is contagious because it is part of a mechanism which serves to synchronise wake/sleep cycles among different members of the social group. (Reference: Provine *et al.*, *Ethology*, 1987, vol. 76, p.10.) *(Dr) A. T. Chamberlain, Department of Human Anatomy, University of Liverpool.*

QUESTION: What are the rules of the game 'Mornington Crescent'?

□ I HAVE no proof, but I believe that 'Mornington Crescent' is derived from the game 'Finchley Central' which was invented by John Conway (now Professor of Mathematics at Princeton University, but then a lecturer in Cambridge) around 20 years ago. 'Finchley Central' was invented as an example of a game with extremely simple rules which defies conventional game-theoretic analysis, and its rules are as follows: two players alternately name stations on the London Underground, and the first one to say 'Finchley Central' is the winner. However, in order to achieve a perfect win (which is worth infinitely more than an ordinary win), you must say 'Finchley Central' immediately before your opponent was going to say it. It seems quite probable that this game evolved into 'Mornington Crescent' as played on 'I'm Sorry, I Haven't a Clue' but I have no information about the route by which it got there. *(Dr) P. T. Johnstone, Dept of Pure Mathematics and Mathematical Statistics, Cambridge.*

□ THE origins of 'Mornington Crescent' have been most

reliably traced to the old Gerry's Club in London's West End (now under new management). Among the regulars to whom Gerry's in the sixties was not so much a haunt as a home, the writer John Junkin has claimed authorship of the game. Nowadays, however, even Junkin is slow to divulge the rules, and the determined enquirer must have time and money on his side (about £20 ought to do it). For those who will stop at nothing, N. Stovold's *Rules And Origins* may be begged or stolen; but it has been out of print for years, and the British Library has drawn a blank on it. More fruitfully, though, the regulars of 'I'm Sorry I Haven't a Clue' on Radio 4 can still be heard playing the original game to a high standard of elegance and cunning. Indeed, William Rushton's lethal mastery of Junkin's Parallel remains a joy to behold. I fear, though, that this is as much as can be said in print. The truth is that 'Mornington Crescent', like poker, can be played but seldom explained; its rules can be learnt but never taught; and its beauty should be noted but never queried.
Jon Magnusson, Producer, BBC Radio Light Entertainment, London W1.

□ WHEN playing the underground version of 'Mornington Crescent' it is vital to remember that it was quite difficult to alight at 'Mornington Crescent' as most trains did not stop there.
C. S. Mence, New Malden, Surrey.

□ THIS question is really too tiresome to bother with a full answer, and in any case Samantha (the scorer) is probably the only person fully qualified to answer it in full. The questioner must just listen more carefully and work out the rules for himself.
Justin Downing, Sheffield.

QUESTION: Who originally said or wrote 'Man made God in his own image'?

☐ THE *Penguin Dictionary of Quotations* records that Voltaire wrote in *Le Sottisier:* 'Si Dieu nous a fait à son image, nous le lui avons bien rendu' (If God made us in His image, we have certainly returned the compliment). *John Wymer, Bridport, Dorset.*

☐ XENOPHANES of Kolophon, a sceptic and founder of the Eleatic school, wrote around the sixth century BC that 'Men imagine gods to be born, and to have clothes and voices and shapes like theirs ... the gods of the Ethiopians are black and flat-nosed, the gods of the Thracians are red-haired and blue eyed. Yet if oxen and horses and lions had hands ... horses would fashion their gods as horses, oxen as oxen. Homer and Hesiod have ascribed to gods all things that are a shame and disgrace among men; theft, adultery, deceit and other lawless acts.' Although Xenophanes did not coin precisely the phrase in question, it most certainly derived from this observation. *Ulrig Brookmyre, London SW 11.*

QUESTION: Why do fishmongers, not butchers, deal in game? Why isn't a butcher a 'meatmonger'?

☐ As far as I know there is no reason why a butcher should not sell game, and I have seen some who do, but the answer to the second part of the question can be found in the *Oxford English Dictionary*. 'Butcher' is derived from the Old French *bochier*, literally 'dealer in goat's flesh', and is defined by the *Oxford English Dictionary* as 'one whose trade is slaughtering large tame animals for food; one who kills such animals and sells their flesh'. A 'monger', on the other hand, is one who is a 'dealer, trader, trafficker'. He does not catch or kill his product but is the agent for the producer. Though modern butchers do not necessarily slaughter the animals they sell, the traditional name has carried on and, as the *OED*

puts it, 'sometimes denotes a tradesman who merely deals in meat'. The term which corresponds to 'fishmonger' is not, in fact, 'meatmonger' but 'fleshmonger' *(OED)*. Unfortunately this word is open to ribald use, as in *Measure For Measure*, V. i. 337.
(Dr) L. C. Knowles, Rickmansworth, Herts.

QUESTION: Who first faded out at the end of a record, rather than having a proper ending?

☐ THE first person to fade the end of a piece of music was Gustav Holst. In the last movement of his *Planets* suite he used the gradually fading sound of a female choir to evoke the immensity of outer space. As this was written in 1915 before the introduction of electrical recording, he asked his singers to walk slowly into the distance while still singing, or for a door to be gradually closed between them and the audience. In this astonishing movement Holst anticipated the later electronic fade-out, but had in fact already used the idea as early as 1905 in his settings of songs from Tennyson's *The Princess*.
Michael Short, Bradford-on-Avon, Wilts.

☐ JOHANN Strauss (father) composed the Radetzky March in 1848, in honour of Field Marshal Radetzky who put down Italian patriots in Milan in the same year. The fifes fade out at the end, marching away into the distance. Other members of the Strauss family use the same device (e.g. Perpetuum Mobile).
G. H. Shackleton, Reading, Berks.

☐ ACCORDING to Nick Tosches in his book, *Country*, the first record to have a fade-out was 'The New Call of the Freaks', recorded by Luis Russell, the jazz musician, on 6 September, 1929. This version of a tune previously recorded by Russell fades out on the added chanted refrain: 'Stick out your can, here comes the garbage man.'
David Rothon, London SW12.

☐ YOUR correspondent's source is incorrect: although Luis Russell's 'The New Call of the Freaks' contains the refrain he quotes, the recording actually ends with guitar and vibes. As I believe, however, that the effect is achieved by nothing more technical than the musicians' progressively softer playing, this still leaves the title of 'first electronically achieved fade' up for grabs. Such trifles aside, Russell led one of the great bands of the late Twenties and early Thirties: his fiery version of 'Panama', admired by Philip Larkin, is described in loving detail in Humphrey Lyttelton's *The Best of Jazz*, Volume 1.
Anthony Teague, Enfield, Middx.

☐ DUKE Ellington's 'Showboat shuffle' (from 1935) fades away at the end but I think it was Count Basie, in the late 1930s, who started the fashion. I assume it caught on because it was a convenient way around the problem of how to end a piece. And perhaps some jazz records were faded out simply because musicians exceeded the three to 3½-minute time limit of the old 78s.
Sidney Evans, Chirk, Clwyd.

☐ FADE-outs became widespread in the United States as the result of a trade survey in the early 50s. This showed that when records were played on juke-boxes, people felt more inclined to replay a record that faded out because it left a subconscious feeling that you hadn't completely heard it. The importance of the 'juke-box factor' has never been as potent in Britain, but in the States its earning capacity has always been considerable. After the creation of the fade-out ending, the only other innovation to stimulate juke-box plays was pioneered by the Chess-Checker Record Company of Chicago, who developed a new groove-cutting technique for their 45s, which ensured that when played on juke-boxes, they were one-third louder than all other records in the machine.
Dave Godin, Sheffield.

☐ THE fade has been used as an effect for many years, but it is especially suited to pop numbers, which usually consist of, or develop into, repetition of a single monotonous phrase. In consequence, the device was seized on by the groups, most of which were able to produce (one hesitates to say compose) such phrases but lacked the musical talent to bring them to an end.
David Carlé, Guildford.

QUESTION: When Napoleon called us a nation of shopkeepers what was the French word he used?

☐ NAPOLEON'S remark (if indeed he ever made it) is recorded by B. B. E. O'Meara in his work, *Napoleon at St Helena:* 'L'Angleterre est une nation de boutiquiers.' The idea was not original, and had already been expressed by no less an authority than Adam Smith, among others.
Edwin Hudson, St Albans, Herts.

QUESTION: Why do we hear the sound of the sea when we hold a shell to our ear?

☐ WHEN we hold a shell to our ear, we hear our own blood rushing through the blood vessels in our ear. The shape of the shell provides a simple sort of echo chamber, and the opening in the shell allows other sounds to be almost shut out when we hold the shell to our ear. It is not just sea-shells that allow us to hear the 'sea'. We can achieve the same effect with hollow animal horns, tin cups, and ... pyramids. The King's chamber in the Great Pyramid of Cheops at Giza, Cairo, acts as a large echo-chamber, and is also incredibly well sound-proofed. If ever you could spend some time alone in the chamber and in the pyramid, you would, after about 15 minutes of

total silence, hear a very loud rushing noise, like the sound of a waterfall at the end of a deep, quiet valley. This sound is the sound of the blood in your body, especially close to your ears. The same sound you hear when you hold a sea-shell to your ear.
Andrew Weston-Webb, London SW 8.

QUESTION: Who said 'There but for the grace of God go I' – and of whom was it said?

☐ JOHN Bradford, seeing a group of criminals being led out to execution, is reported to have said 'There, but for the grace of God, goes John Bradford.' Bradford was a Protestant reformer who was born, like the *Guardian*, in Manchester. In the 1550s he was prebendary of St Paul's Cathedral and on the accession of Queen Mary he was arrested and accused of preaching seditious sermons. He was eventually burnt at the stake in June 1555.
Geoffrey T. Brown, Widnes, Cheshire.

☐ THIS quotation is ascribed to the Italian saint, Philip Neri (1515-1595). He was the founder of the Congregation of the Oratory. He had a special gift to achieve great spiritual conversions and nourish people's minds and hearts in apparently humorous ways which, while producing laughter, also purified the soul. He was well aware of his own weaknesses and that 'were it not for the grace of God' he, too, could be seeking God's pardon in the Sacrament of Reconciliation: in fact his behaviour could well become very similar to that of his penitents!
Rev. Brother L. Ryan, St Joseph's College, Stoke-on-Trent.

QUESTION: Can anyone recollect a children's story that was broadcast on the Home Service in the late

1950s? The storyline was similar to *Cinderella*, but all the characters were mice.

☐ IT IS possible that the story was 'Mossy Green Theatre' by Mary Dunn, about a little girl called Jane who made a theatre out of sticks and moss in the roots of a tree in the New Forest and found it being used for a production of *Cinderella* by the birds and animals who lived there. The title role was to be played by Gloria la Souris, a white mouse, but after an accident during rehearsals when she broke a leg, the part was taken by Binnie Small, an unknown field mouse.
(Mrs) Perry Bell, Reading, Berks.

☐ READERS may be interested to know of a book called *BBC Children's Hour: a celebration of those magical years* by Wallace Grevatt (The Book Guild, 1988) which lovingly documents all the programmes put out as part of the BBC 'Children's Hour' from 1922 to 1964. Browsing through this, which is arranged chronologically, one's eye may alight upon a likely title. It should be available in any good public library.
Sheila Ray, Llanbrynmair, Powys.

QUESTION: What is the origin of the word Subbuteo?

☐ THE popular flick football game was originally to be patented under the title 'Hobby'. This was disallowed, so the inventor (a keen ornithologist) brought on his substitute: the Latin name for the Hobby (a type of falcon). Thus Subbuteo kicked off just after the Second World War, on old army blankets. These facts were gleaned from Channel Four's recent broadcast of the Subbuteo World Cup, memorable for revealing that this sport has an

unimpressive off-the-pitch violence record, just like the real thing.
Peter Wilson, Gateshead.

☐ THE origin of Subbuteo is part of trade mark folklore. It was the inventor's original intention to call it 'Hobby', but descriptive trade marks are not registrable.
R. G. Pratt, Lecturer in Trade Mark Law, Anglia Higher Education College, Chelmsford, Essex.

QUESTION: How many islands are there in the British Isles?

☐ THE islands of all sorts and sizes are, in the true sense of the word, innumerable. But considering only those which are 0.2 hectares (half an acre) or more in area and are islands at all states of the tide, the British Isles total about 4,400; of these about 210 are inhabited. An additional 6,100 are islands at high tide, consequently not all at the same time. The foregoing figures include respectively about 850, 70 and 1,000 which are in the Republic of Ireland.
Brian Adams (retired hydrographic officer), London SW6.

QUESTION: Who says that tea should be made with boiling water? Why not 90°C, for instance?

☐ WATER at boiling point maximises the penetrating power of the liquid and enables it to dissolve out from the leaf the flavour and colour which is essential to a good cup of tea. Water below boiling point cannot do this.
Len Snow, Wembley, Middx.

☐ MY physics teacher at school told me that mountaineers on Everest were unable to make a decent brew because the reduced atmospheric pressure at high altitude lowered the boiling point of water to between 60°C and 70°C.

At sea level (or thereabouts, where most of us drink our tea), water boils at 100°C. By using the hottest possible water to make the tea we get a quicker, stronger brew and the tea is still nice and hot when drunk.
P. H. Johnstone, London SE24.

QUESTION: Is there any reference in authentic Jewish historical records to the massacre of male infants up to two years of age between 8 BC and AD 6?

☐ THERE is no trace of this story anywhere except for the one reference in Matthew's gospel. It is not mentioned, for example, by the Jewish historian Josephus. The story is not historically impossible. Herod was a ruthless killer who murdered a number of his own children. Had he heard rumours of a child destined to supplant him it would have been entirely in character for him to have acted in this way. Since the number of children involved would have been quite small, the lack of reference to this story in other sources is not of itself decisive.

On the other hand Matthew, in his stories about the infancy of Jesus, seeks to present the truth about Jesus through what are closer to being meditations on Old Testament texts rather than simple bald historical statements. Throughout his gospel he seeks to show that Jesus is the New Moses. Here, just as Pharaoh slaughtered the children before the birth of Moses, so now Herod does the same before the birth of Jesus. In both cases, however, God foils the plans of tyrants and proceeds to liberate his people. In probability therefore the origin of this story is not history but reflection on an Old Testament text.
(Rev.) Martin Camroux, Birkenhead, Wirral.

☐ THE Jewish-Roman historian, Josephus, gives a fascinating, if partisan account of Herod's career in The Jewish War. Herod is portrayed as a brilliant ruler but a ruthless and brutal man who ordered the execution of his favourite wife, Mariamne in a fit of jealousy. He had no compunction in torturing and murdering anyone he believed was implicated in real or imaginary plots against him. No one was safe – brother, mother-in-law, sisters-in-law, brothers-in-law. His relationships with his numerous family (10 known wives and 15 children) were so troubled that it was said that it was safer to be Herod's pig (in view of his conformity to Jewish dietary law) than his son. His two sons by Mariamne were strangled and he ordered the execution of his eldest son and heir only five days before his own death. Herod was obviously aware of how unpopular he was with his subjects and Josephus describes how he planned one last monstrous outrage. As he lay dying in agony, he locked up the leading men from towns and villages all over Judaea in the hippodrome with instructions that they were to be butchered as soon as he died. He thus hoped to ensure that there would be weeping and mourning at his death instead of the expected wild rejoicings. Happily, his sister made sure the prisoners were released before they could be murdered. A man as callous as this would not hesitate to massacre a few baby boys in an insignificant little village if he thought one of them might be a threat to him.
Linda Holmes, Cottingham, N. Humberside.

☐ THE story is part of the myth that grew up around the concept of Jesus as the Messiah, the destined King of Israel. A similar slaughter was rumoured to have been carried out by King Arthur, and there are parallels in African traditions. The idea, a very ancient one, is that the Old King, hoping to be immortal, goes to any length to prevent the conception, birth and survival of his successor. Behind this, no doubt, is the subterranean enmity of fathers towards the sons who will grow to manhood as they themselves decline towards death.

C. C. Wrigley, Lewes, E. Sussex.

QUESTION: *Oxford English Dictionary*: 'Staggers – disease of brain and spinal cord, esp in horses and cattle.' First recorded usage: 1577. Any connection with BSE??

☐ STAGGERS is caused by hypomagnesaemia (a drop in the magnesium level of the blood). In cattle the disease is commonest in the spring and is associated with grazing lush pasture. There is absolutely no connection with BSE, although some of the symptoms, such as muscle tremor, hyperexcitability and loss of co-ordination, are very similar. The disease is of short duration compared to BSE, where the symptoms show a progressive worsening over several weeks. Treating by injection of magnesium salts is usually extremely effective within a very short time. The similarity of the symptoms is responsible for the increased reporting of suspect cases of BSE in the spring.

G. P. David, BVSc MRCVS, Shrewsbury.

QUESTION: Why 15, 30, 40 (not 45) in tennis?

☐ ORIGINALLY, a points scoring system was introduced, based on the quarters of a clock, in minutes, probably to avoid confusing point scores with game scores. This provided a neat, cyclic '15-30-45-game' system. However, the three-syllable '45' proved too much of a mouthful, and was soon abbreviated to '40', and has stayed as such ever since. (Ironically the estranged 'five' has made a comeback at club level, as an abbreviation itself, for '15' when the players themselves are keeping score.)

Peter J. Phillips, London E6.

QUESTION: Why does Pernod go cloudy when mixed with water? Dettol does the same but is not so delicious.

☐ WHEN water is added to Pernod (or Ricard), the alcohol concentration is reduced sharply; this causes the precipitation of a number of compounds in the terpene family which are normally held in solution by the very high alcohol concentration. The terpene family includes molecules such as thujone (from wormwood), fenchone (from fennel) and camphor. Thujone was a primary ingredient in absinthe, and was the main reason for it being so poisonous; not surprisingly, wormwood is not used in the production of Pernod and Ricard. There is an excellent article on the chemistry of absinthe and the terpene family in the June, 1989 edition of the magazine *Scientific American*.
Andrew J. Stewart, Hull.

☐ IT IS a chemical reaction caused by the essential oils and resins from the herbal extracts (there are 15 different herbs in Pernod including star anise, fennel, spinach, coriander and camomile) which are precipitated out of the alcohol and remain in suspension in the water to form an emulsion.
Simon Hesketh, Product Group Manager (Pernod), Campbell Distillers Ltd, Brentford, Middx.

QUESTION: Who was the Bill Bailey who kept being urged to come home?

☐ BILL Bailey, a music teacher of Jackson, Michigan, was an habitué of the Whistler Bar where songwriter Hughie Cannon played piano. The frequent pleasure in drinking was as frequently marred for Bill Bailey by his wife Sarah nagging him when he arrived home late.

Bailey confided this sorrow to Cannon inspiring him to write the song, 'Bill Bailey Won't You Please Come Home', published in 1902. In 1910 Sarah divorced Bill Bailey. We can presume Bill continued drinking, his happiness unhampered, until he died in 1954. Sarah, who claimed the song helped break up the marriage, lived to enjoy – if someone who disapproves of drinking-places can – her 100th birthday in 1973. I would think 'Bill Bailey ...' is the only song by Hughie Cannon ever performed now. However, he specialised in songs with titles like 'Just Because She Made Dem Goo-goo Eyes So', perhaps, that is just as well. Most of this information can be found in Eric Townley's *Tell Your Story: A Dictionary of Jazz and Blues.*
Tommy Moulds, Glasgow.

INDEX